Open Advice

Lydia Pintscher (Editor)

Open Advice

FOSS: What We Wish We Had Known When We Started

Visit `http://www.open-advice.org` to download this book as PDF or eBook and receive additional information.

ISBN: 978-1-105-51493-7

for giants
and those who will stand on their shoulders

Foreword

This is a book about community and technology. It is a book that represents a collective effort, much like the technology we build together. And if this is in fact your first encounter with our community, you may find it strange to think of a community as the driving force behind technology. Isn't technology built by large corporations? Actually, for us it is almost the other way around.

The authors in this book are all members of what you could label the software freedom community. A group of people sharing the fundamental experience that software is more empowering, more useful, more flexible, more controllable, more just, more encompassing, more sustainable, more efficient, more secure and ultimately just better when it comes with four fundamental freedoms: to use, study, share and improve the software.

And while there is now an increasing number of communities that have left behind the requirement for geographical proximity by means of virtual communication, it was this community that pioneered that new age.

In fact, the Internet and the Free Software Community[1] were co-dependent developments. As the Internet grew, our community could grow with it, but without the values and technology of our community, I have no doubts that the Internet would not have become the all-encompassing network that we now see enabling people and groups around the world.

Until today, our software runs most of the Internet, and you will know at least some of it, such as Mozilla Firefox, OpenOffice.org, Linux, and perhaps even GNOME or KDE. But our technology may also be hidden inside your TV, your wireless router, your ATM, even your radio, security system or battleships. It is literally everywhere.

[1] For me, Open Source is one aspect of that community which articulated itself in 1998, so quite some time after the Internet came about. But please feel free to replace Free Software by Open Source in your head if that is your preferred terminology.

It was essential in enabling some of the large corporations that you know, such as Google, Facebook, Twitter and others. None of these could have achieved so much in such a short time if it were not for the power of software freedom that allowed them to stand on the shoulders of those who came before.

But there are many smaller companies that live from, with, and for Free Software, including my own, Kolab Systems. Active partaking in the community in good faith and standing has become a critical success factor for all of us. And this is true even for the large ones, as Oracle has involuntarily demonstrated during and after its takeover of Sun Microsystems.

But it is important to understand that our community is **not** anti-commercial. We enjoy our work, and many of us have made it their profession for their livelihood and mortgage. So when we say community, we mean students, entrepreneurs, developers, artists, documentation writers, teachers, tinkerers, businessmen, sales people, volunteers and users.

Yes, users. Even if you did not realize it or "never signed up for no community," you in fact are already *almost* part of ours. The question is whether you'll choose to participate actively.

And this is what sets us apart from the monoculture behemoths, the gated communities, the corporate owned walled gardens of companies like Apple, Microsoft and others. Our doors are open. So is our advice. And your potential. There is no limit as to what you can become – it purely depends on your personal choice as it has depended for each of us.

So if you are not yet part of our community, or simply curious, this book provides a good starting point. And if you are already an active participant, this book might provide you with insights into a few facets and perspectives that are new to you.

Because this book contains important grains of that implicit knowledge which we usually build and transfer inside our sub-communities that work on different technologies. This knowledge typically trickles down from experienced contributors to less experienced ones, which is why it seems very obvious and natural to those socialized in our community.

This knowledge and culture of how to shape collaboration allows us to build outstanding technology in small, distributed teams across language, country and cultural barriers around the world, outperforming much larger development teams in some of the world's largest corporations.

All the people writing in this book are such experienced contributors in one, sometimes several areas. They have grown to become teachers and mentors. Over the course of the past 15 years or so I had the pleasure of getting to know most of them, working with many, and the privilege to call some of them friends.

Because as Kevin Ottens rightly said during the Desktop Summit 2011 in Berlin: "Community building is family and friendship building."

So it is in fact with a profound sense of gratitude that I can say there is no other community I would rather be part of, and I look forward to hopefully seeing you at one or the other upcoming conference.

— Georg Greve

Zürich, Switzerland; 20. August 2011

Georg Greve initiated the Free Software Foundation Europe in 2000 and was its founding president until 2009. During this time he was responsible for building up and designing many of FSFE's activities such as the Fellowship, the policy or legal work, and has worked intensively with many communities. Today he continues this work as shareholder and CEO of Kolab Systems AG, a fully Free Software company. For his accomplishments in Free Software and Open Standards Georg Greve was awarded the Federal Cross of Merit on ribbon by the Federal Republic of Germany on 18 December 2009.

Thank You!

This book would not have been possible without the support of each of the authors and the following people, who helped make it happen:

- Anne Gentle (editing)
- Bernhard Reiter (editing)
- Celeste Lyn Paul (editing)
- Daniel Molkentin (layout)
- Debajyoti Datta (website)
- Irina Rempt (editing)
- Jeff Mitchell (editing)
- Mans Rullgard (editing)
- Noirin Plunkett (editing)
- Oregon State University Open Source Lab (website hosting)
- Stuart Jarvis (editing)
- Supreet Pal Singh (website)
- Saransh Sinha (website)
- Vivek Prakash (editing)
- Will Kahn-Greene (editing)

Contents

Part I.

Ideas and Innovation

1. Code First

Armijn Hemel

Armijn Hemel has been using free software since 1994, when his brother came home with a stack of floppies with an early version of FreeBSD. A year later the switch to Linux was made and he has been using Unix(-like) systems ever since then, both at home, during his studies at Utrecht University and at work. Since 2005, Armijn has been part of the core team of gpl-violations.org and has his own consultancy (Tjaldur Software Governance Solutions) specialized in detection and resolution of GPL license violations.

Back in 1999 I was just getting started in FLOSS activism. I had already been using Linux and FreeBSD for a number of years then, but I was merely a user and I wanted to actually contribute something back. The best way I thought for contributing back was to write code. I could not find any existing project I would be comfortable working on, so I decided to start my own project. In hindsight the reason why I did that was probably a mixture of various things. One factor was insecurity whether or not my code was actually good enough to be accepted in an existing project (I was, and still am, no brilliant programmer) and with your own project that is not much of an issue. The second reason is probably youthful arrogance.

My idea was to make a presentation program, which would fancy more of the advanced (or, annoying, if you wish) features of PowerPoint. Back in that time there was no OpenOffice.org and choices were pretty limited to LaTeX and Magicpoint, which are more tailored to delivering text content, than to showing whirly effects. I wanted to make the program cross platform and back then I thought Java would be the best choice for this. The idea was to make a presentation program, written in Java, which would have support for all those whirly effects. I made up my mind and started the project.

Infrastructure-wise everything was there: there was a mailing list, there was a website, there was source code control (CVS). But there was no actual code for people to work on. The only things I had were some ideas of what I wanted to do, an itch to scratch and the right buzzwords. I actually wanted people to join in creating this program and make it a truly collaborative project.

I started making designs (with some newly acquired UML knowledge) and sent them around. Nothing happened. I tried to get people involved, but collaboratively working on a design is very hard (besides, it is probably not the best way to create software in the first place). After a while I gave up and the project silently died, without ever producing a single line of code. Every month I was reminded by the mailing list software that the project once existed, so I asked it to be taken offline.

I learned a very valuable, but somewhat painful, lesson: when you announce something and when you want people to get involved in your project, at least make sure there is some code available. It does not have to be all finished, it is OK if it is rough (in the beginning that is), but at least show that there is a basis for people to work with and improve upon. Otherwise your project will go where many many projects, including my own failed project, have gone: into oblivion.

I eventually found my niche to help advance FLOSS, by making sure that the legal underpinnings of FLOSS are tight through the gpl-violations.org project. In retrospect I have never used, nor missed, the whirly effects in presentation programs and found them to be increasingly irritating and distracting too much from the content. I am happily using LaTeX beamer and occasionally (and less happily) OpenOffice.org/LibreOffice to make presentations.

2. Everyone Else Might Be Wrong, But Probably Not

Evan Prodromou

Evan Prodromou is the founder of Wikitravel, StatusNet and the Open Source social network Identi.ca. He has participated in Open Source software for 15 years as a developer, documentation writer, and occasional bomb-throwing crank. He lives in Montreal, Quebec.

The most important characteristic of the Open Source project founder, in the first weeks or months before releasing their software into the world, is mule-headed persistence in the face of overwhelming factual evidence. If your software is so important, why has someone else not written it already? Maybe it is not even possible. Maybe nobody else wants what you are making. Maybe you are not good enough to make it. Maybe someone else already did, and you are just not good enough at Googling to find it.

Keeping the faith through that long, dark night is hard; only the most pig-headed, opinionated, stubborn people make it through. And we get to exercise all our most strongly-held programmer's opinions. What is the best programming language to use? Application architecture? Coding standards? Icon colors? Software license? Version control system? If you are the only one who works on (or knows about!) the project, you get to decide, unilaterally.

When you eventually launch, though, that essential characteristic of stubborn determination and strong opinion becomes a detriment, not a benefit. Once you have launched, you will need exactly the opposite skill to make compromises to make your software more useful to other people. And a lot of those compromises will feel really wrong.

It is hard to take input from "outsiders" (e.g., people who are not you). First, because they focus on such trivial, unimportant things – your variable naming convention, say, or the placement of particular buttons. And second, because they are invariably wrong – after all, if what you have done is not the right way to do it, you would not have done it that way in the first place. If your way was not the right way, why would your code be popular?

But "wrong" is relative. If making a "wrong" choice makes your software more accessible for end users, or for downstream developers, or for administrators or packagers, is that not really right?

And the nature of these kind of comments and contributions is usually negative. Community feedback is primarily reactive, which means it is primarily critical. When was the last time you filed a bug report to say, "I really like the organization of the hashtable.c module." or "Great job on laying out that sub-sub-sub-menu."? People give feedback because they do not like the way things work right now with your software. They also might not be diplomatic in delivering that news.

It is hard to respond to this kind of feedback positively. Sometimes, we flame posters on our development mailing lists, or close bug reports with a sneer and a WONTFIX. Worse, we withdraw into our cocoon, ignoring outside suggestions or feedback, cuddling up with the comfortable code that fits our preconceptions and biases perfectly.

If your software is just for you, you can keep the codebase and surrounding infrastructure as a personal playground. But if you want your software to be used, to mean something to other people, to (maybe) change the world, then you are going to need to build up a thriving, organic community of users, core committers, admins and add-on developers. People need to feel like they own the software, in the same way that you do.

It is hard to remember that each one of those dissenting voices is the tiny corner of the wedge. Imagine all the people who hear about your software and never bother to try it. Those who download it but never install it. Those who install it, get stuck, and silently give up. And those who do want to give you feedback, but can not find your bug-report system, developers mailing list, IRC channel or personal email address. Given the barriers to getting a message through, there are likely about 100 people who want to see change for every one person to get the message through. So listening to those voices, when they do reach you, is critical.

The project leader is responsible for maintaining the vision and purpose of the software. We can not vacillate, swinging back and forth based on this or that email from random users. And if there is a core principle at stake, then, of course, it is important to hold that core steady. No one else but the project leader can do that.

But we have to think: are there non-core issues that can make your software more accessible or usable? Ultimately the measure of our work is in how we reach people, how our software is used, and what it is used for. How much does our personal idea about what is "right" really matter to the project and to the community? How much is just what the leader likes, personally? If those non-core issues exist, reduce the friction, respond to the demand, and make the changes. It is going to make the project better for everyone.

Part II.

Research

3. Out of the Lab, into the Wild: Growing Open Source Communities around Academic Projects

Markus Krötzsch

Markus Krötzsch is a post-doctoral researcher at the Department of Computer Science of the University of Oxford. He obtained his Ph.D. from the Institute of Applied Informatics and Formal Description Methods (AIFB) of the Karlsruhe Institute of Technology (KIT) in 2010. His research interest is the intelligent automatic processing of information, ranging from the foundations of formal knowledge representation to application areas like the Semantic Web. He is the lead developer of the successful Semantic Web application platform Semantic MediaWiki, co-editor of the W3C OWL 2 specification, chief maintainer of the semanticweb.org community portal, and co-author of the textbook Foundations of Semantic Web Technologies.

Academic researchers develop large amounts of software, be it for validating a hypothesis, for illustrating a new approach, or merely as a tool to aid some study. In most cases, a small focused prototype does the job, and it is disposed quickly after the focus of research moves on. However, once in a while, a novel approach or upcoming technology bears the potential to really change the way in which a problem is solved. Doing so promises professional reputation, commercial success, and the personal gratification of realizing the full potential of a new idea. The researcher who made this discovery then is tempted to go beyond a prototype towards a *product* that is actually used – and is faced by a completely new set of practical problems.

The Fear of the User

Frederick P. Brooks, Jr., in one of his famous essays on software engineering, gives a good picture of the efforts related to maintaining real software, and warns us of the user:

> "The total cost of maintaining a widely used program is typically 40 percent or more of the cost of developing it. Surprisingly, this cost is strongly affected by the number of users. More users find more bugs."[1]

While this figure might well be different in today's environment, the basic observation is still true, and may even have been aggravated by the use of instantaneous global communication. Even worse, more users not only find more actual bugs, but also articulate more wishes in general. Be it a genuine error, a feature request, or merely a fundamental misunderstanding of the software's operation, the typical user request is far from being a technically precise bug report. And each request demands the attention of the developers, consuming precious time that is not available to actually write code.

The analytical mind of the researcher foresees this issue, and, in its natural struggle to prevent a gloomy future in customer care, may develop an outright *fear of the user*. In the worst case, this may lead to a decision against the whole project, in a weaker form it may still lead researchers to practically hide brilliant software products from potential users. More than once have I heard researchers saying: "We don't need more visibility, we are getting enough emails already!" And indeed, there are cases where the communication effort related to a software tool exceeds the effort that a researcher can invest without abandoning her main job.

Often, however, this tragic outcome could easily have been prevented. Brooks could hardly foresee this. When he wrote his essays, users were indeed customers, and software maintenance was part of

[1] Frederick P. Brooks, Jr.: The Mythical Man-Month. Essays on Software Engineering. Anniversary Edition. Addison-Wesley, 1995.

the product they purchased. A balance had to be found between development effort, market demand, and pricing. This is still the case for many commercial software products today, but has little to do with the reality of small-scale Open Source development. Typical OSS users do not pay for the service they receive. Their attitude accordingly is not that of a demanding customer, but more often that of a grateful and enthusiastic supporter. No small part of the art of successful OSS maintenance is turning this enthusiasm into much needed support, balancing the increase in user interest with an increase in user contribution.

Recognizing that Open Source users are not just "customers who don't pay" is an important insight. But it must not lead us to overestimate their potential. The optimistic counterpart of the irrational fear of the user is the belief that active and supportive Open Source communities grow naturally, based merely on the license that was chosen for publishing code. This grave error of judgement is still surprisingly common, and has sealed the doom of many attempts of creating open communities.

Sowing and Reaping

The plural of "user" is not "community." While the former may grow in numbers, the latter does not grow by itself, or grows wildly without yielding the hoped-for support for the project. The task of the project maintainer who seeks to benefit from the users' raw energy therefore resembles that of a gardener who needs to prepare a fertile ground, plant and water the seedlings, and possibly prune undesired shoots before being able to reap the fruits. Compared to the rewards the overall effort is little, but it is vital to do the right things, at the right time.

Preparing the Technical Ground Building a community starts even before the first user appears. Already the choice of the programming language determines how many people will be able to deploy and debug our code. Objective Caml might be a beautiful language, but using Java instead will increase the amount of potential users and contributors by orders of magnitude. Developers thus must compromise, since the most widespread technology is rarely most efficient or elegant. This can be a particularly hard step for researchers who often prefer superiority of language design. When working on Semantic MediaWiki, I have often been asked why in the world we would use PHP when server-side Java would be so much cleaner and more efficient. Comparing the community size of Semantic MediaWiki with similar Java-based efforts may answer this question. This example also illustrates that the target audience determines the best choice of base technology. The developer herself should have the necessary insight to make a most opportunistic decision.

Thoroughly Working the Ground A related issue is the creation of readable and well documented code from the very start. In an academic environment, some software projects are touched by many temporary contributors. Changing staff and student projects may deteriorate code quality. I remember a small software project at TU Dresden that had been maintained quite well by a student assistant. After he had left it was found that his code was thoroughly documented – in Turkish. A researcher can only be a part-time programmer, so special discipline is needed to enforce the extra work needed for accessible code. The reward will be a much greater chance of informed bug reports, useful patches, or even external developers later on.

Spreading the Seeds of Communities Inexperienced Open Source developers often think it as a big step to publish their code openly. In reality nobody else will notice. To attract users and contributors alike one has to spread the word. The public communication of a real project should at least involve announcements for every new release. Mailing lists are probably the best channels for this. Some social skill is needed to find the balance between annoying spam and shy understatement. Projects that are motivated by the honest conviction that they will help users to solve real problems should be easy to advertise respectably. Users will quickly notice the difference between shameless advertising and useful information. Obviously, active announcements should wait until the project is ready. This does not only include its actual code but also its homepage and basic usage documentation.

Throughout its lifetime, the project should be mentioned in all *appropriate* places, including web sites (start with your homepage!), presentations, scientific papers, online discussions. One cannot appreciate enough the power of the single link that leads a later main contributor to his first visit of the project's homepage. Researchers should not forget to also publicize their software outside of their immediate academic community. Other researchers are rarely the best basis for an active community.

Providing Spaces to Grow Trivially easy, yet often neglected is the duty of project maintainers to provide for the communication spaces that communities can grow in. If a project has no dedicated mailing list, then all support requests will be sent privately to the maintainer. If there is no public bug tracker, bug reports will be fewer and less helpful. Without a world-editable wiki for user documentation, the developer is left with extending and refining the documentation continuously. If the development trunk of the source code is not accessible, then users will not be able to check the latest version before complaining about bugs. If the code repository is inherently closed, then it is impossible to admit external contributors. All of this infrastructure is offered for free by a number of service providers. Not all forms of interaction might be desired, e.g. there are reasons to keep the group of developers closed. But it would be foolish to expect support from a community without even preparing the basic spaces for this.

Encouraging and Controlling Growth Inexperienced developers often are concerned that opening up mailing lists, forums, and wikis for users will require a lot of additional maintenance. It rarely does, but some basic activities are of course necessary. It starts with *rigorously enforcing* the use of public communication. Users need to be educated to ask questions publicly, to look up the documentation before asking, and to report bugs in the tracker instead of via email. I tend to reject all private support requests, or to forward the answers to public lists. This also ensures that solutions are available on the web for future users to find. In any case, users should be thanked explicitly for all forms of contribution – many enthusiastic and well-meaning people are needed for building a healthy community.

When a certain density of users is reached, support starts to happen from user to user. This is always a magical moment for a project, and a sure sign that it is on a good path. Ideally, the core maintainers should still provide support for tricky questions, but at some point certain users will take the lead in discussions, and it is important to thank them (personally) and to involve them further in the project. Conversely, unhealthy developments must be stopped where possible, and in particular aggressive behavior can be a real danger to community development. Likewise, not all well-meant enthusiasm is productive, and it is often necessary to say no, friendly but clearly, to prevent feature creep.

The Future is Open

Building an initial community around a project is an important part of transforming a research prototype into a grown Open Source software. If it succeeds, there are many options for further developing the project, depending on the goals of the project maintainer and community. Some general directions include:

- Continuing to grow and develop the project and its OSS community, enlarging the core team of developers and maintainers, and eventually making it independent of its academic origin.

This may involve further community activities (e.g. dedicated events) and maybe establishing organizational support.

- Founding a company for commercially exploiting the project based on, e.g., a dual-license or consulting business model. Established tools and vibrant communities are a major asset for a start-up company, and can be beneficial to several business strategies without abandoning the original OSS product.

- Withdrawing from the project. There are many reasons why one may no longer be able to maintain the close affiliation to the project. Having established a healthy open community maximizes the chances that the project can continue independently. In any case, it is much more respectable to make a clear cut than to abandon the project silently, killing it by inactivity until its reach is diminished to the point where no future maintainer can be found.

The shape of the community will be different when working toward one of these principal options. But in each case, the role of the researcher changes in the cause of the project. The initial scientist and coder may turn into a manager or technical director. In this sense, the main difference between an influential OSS project and a perpetual research prototype is not so much the amount of work but the type of work that is required to succeed. Understanding this is part of the success – the only other thing that is needed is an awesome piece of software.

4. Prepare for the Future: Evolution of Teams in FLOSS

Felipe Ortega

Felipe Ortega is a researcher and project manager at Libresoft, a research group at University Rey Juan Carlos (URJC), Spain. Felipe develops novel methodologies to analyze open collaborative communities (like free software projects, Wikipedia and social networks). He has done extensive research with the Wikipedia project and its community of authors. He actively participates in research, promotion and education/training on libre software, especially in the Master on Libre Software at URJC. He is a strong advocate of open educational resources, open access in scientific publishing and open data in science.

In his well-known essay *The Cathedral and the Bazaar*[1], Eric S. Raymond remarks one of the first important lessons that every programmer must learn: "Every good work of software starts by scratching a developer's personal itch". You never realize how certain is this statement unless you experience that situation by yourself. In fact, the majority of FLOSS programmers (if not all) certainly underwent this process as they got their hands dirty in a brand new project, or they join an existing one, eager to help making it better. However, many developers and other participants in FLOSS communities (documentation writers, translators, etc.) usually overlook another important lesson stressed by Raymond a bit later in his essay: "When you lose interest in a program, your last duty to it is to hand it off to a competent successor". This is the central topic I want to cover

[1] `http://www.catb.org/~esr/writings/cathedral-bazaar/cathedral-bazaar`

here. You should think about the future of your project, and the newcomers that one day will take over your work and continue to improve it.

Generational relay

At some point in their lifetime, many FLOSS projects must face a generational relay. Former developers in charge of code maintenance and improvement eventually leave the project and its community, for a wide variety of reasons. These include personal issues, a new job that does not leave them enough free time, starting a new project, switching to a different project that seems more appealing, ... The list can be pretty long.

The study of generational relay (or developer turnover) in FLOSS projects is still an emerging area of study that needs further research to improve our understanding of these situations. In spite of this, some researchers have already collected objective evidence that sheds some light on these processes. In OSS 2006, my colleagues Jesus G. Barahona and Gregorio Robles presented a work entitled "Contributor Turnover in Libre Software Projects". In this work, they show a methodology to identify the most active developers (usually known as core contributors) in different time intervals, over the whole history of a given project. Then, they apply this method to study 21 large projects, in particular GIMP, Mozilla (former instance of the well-known browser) and Evolution. In a nutshell, what they found is that we can identify three types of projects according to their rate of developer turnover:

- Code gods projects: These projects heavily rely on the work of their founders, and there is very little generational relay, or none at all. GIMP falls into this category.

- Projects with multiple generations: Projects like Mozilla show a clear pattern of developer turnover, with new groups of active developers taking over the lead of code development and maintenance from the hands of the previous core contributors.

- Composite projects: Evolution belongs to a third category of projects, showing some rate of turnover but not as evident as in the previous case, mitigated by retention of some core contributors over the project history.

This classification leads us to an obvious question: so, what is the most common pattern found in real FLOSS projects out there? Well, results for the whole set of 21 projects analyzed in this work render a clear conclusion, which is that multiple generations and composite projects are the most common cases found in the FLOSS ecosystem. Only Gnumeric and Mono showed a distinctive pattern of strong retention of former developers, indicating that people contributing to these projects may have more appealing reasons to continue their work for a long time.

Nevertheless, this is not the normal picture. On the contrary, this study gives support for the advice we are considering here, that we should prepare to transfer, at some point in the future, our role and knowledge in the project to the future contributors joining our community.

The knowledge gap

Any person experiencing a significant change in her life must deal with adaption to new conditions. For example, when you quit your job to get another one you prepare yourself for a certain period in which you have to fit in a new place, and integrate yourself in a different working group. Hopefully, after a while you have finally settled down in your new job. But, sometimes, you keep good friends from your old job, and you can meet them again after the move. Maybe then, talking with your former workmates, you can learn what happened with the person recruited to fill your previous position. This seldom occurs in FLOSS projects.

The downside of generational relay in FLOSS projects may come in a very concrete form, namely a knowledge gap. When a former developer leaves the project, and especially if she had an extensive experience in that community, she leaves behind both her tangible and abstract knowledge that may or may not be passed on to subsequent newcomers.

A clear example is source code. Like any product of fine intellectual work (well, at least one should expect that, right?) developers leave a personal imprint whenever they produce new code. Sometimes, you feel eternally in debt to that awesome programmer who wrote neat, elegant code that virtually speaks by itself and is easily maintainable. Other times, the situation is the opposite and you struggle to understand very obscure, unclear code without any comments or hints that can help you.

This is what we tried to measure in 2009, in a research work presented at HICSS 2009. The title is "Using Software Archeology to Measure Knowledge Loss in Software Projects Due to Developer Turnover". In case you were wondering, it has nothing to do with a whip, treasures, temples or thrilling adventures, though it was really entertaining. What we measured (among other things) was the percentage of orphaned code left behind by developers who quit FLOSS projects, and not taken by any of the current developers, yet. In this case, we choose four projects (Evolution, GIMP, Evince and Nautilus) to test our research method. And we found quite interesting results.

Evolution exhibited a somewhat worrying pattern, in the sense that the percentage of orphaned code was growing over time. By 2006, nearly 80% of all source code lines had been abandoned by former developers and remained untouched by the rest of the team. On the contrary, GIMP showed a radically different pattern, with a clear and sustained effort of the development team to reduce the number of orphaned lines of code. By the way, remember that GIMP had already been characterized as a code gods project, and thus benefits from a much more stable development team to undertake this daunting task.

Does this mean that GIMP developers were having a much better experience than Evolution folks? To be honest, we do not know. Nevertheless, we can foresee a clear, predictable risk: the higher the percentage of orphaned code, the larger the effort to maintain the project. Whenever you need to fix a bug, develop a new feature or extend an existing one, you bump into code you had never seen before. Of course you may be a fantastic programmer, but no matter how wonderful you are, GIMP developers do have a clear advantage in this case, since they have someone in the team with precise knowledge about most of the code they need to maintain. In addition, they also work to further reduce the portion of unknown source code over time.

It feels like home

Interestingly, some projects manage to retain users for much longer periods than one could expect. Again, we can find empirical evidence supporting this claim. In OSS 2005, Michlmayr, Robles and González-Barahona presented some relevant results pertaining this aspect. They studied the persistence of participation of software maintainers in Debian, calculating the so-called half-life ratio. This is the time needed for a certain population of maintainers to fall to half of its initial size. The result was that the estimated half-life of Debian maintainers was approximately 7.5 years. In other words, since the study was undertaken over a period of six and a half years (between July 1998 to December 2004), comprising from Debian 2.0 to Debian 3.1 (only stable releases), more than 50% of maintainers of Debian 2.0 were still contributing to Debian 3.1.

Debian has created quite a formal procedure to admit new software maintainers (also known as Debian developers) including the acceptance of the Debian Social Contract and showing good knowledge of Debian Policy. As a result, one would expect to have quite committed contributors. Actually this is the case, since these authors found that packages left behind by former maintainers were usually taken over by other developers staying in the community. Only in those case in which the package was not useful anymore it was simply abandoned. I think we can learn some useful conclusions from these research works:

1. Spend some time to develop the main guidelines of your project. It may start as a single, short document, simply featuring some recommendations and good practices. This should evolve as the project grows, to serve as a learning pill for newcomers to quickly grasp the core values of your team, as well as the main traits of your working style.

2. Force yourself to follow well-known coding standards, good practices and elegant style. Document your code. Include comments to describe sections that might be especially hard to understand. Do not feel that you are wasting your time. In practice, you are being very pragmatic, investing time in the future of your project.

3. If possible, when the time comes for you to quit the project try to make others aware of your decision some time in advance. Make sure they understand which critical parts will need a new maintainer. Ideally, if you are a community, prepare at least a very simple procedure to automate this process and make sure that you do not forget any important point before that person leaves the project (especially if she was a key developer).

4. Keep an eye on the size of orphaned code. If it rises too rapidly, or it reaches a significant proportion of your project, it is a clear indication that you will be running into trouble very soon, especially if the number of bug reports grows or you plan to revamp your code with a serious refactoring.

5. Always ensure that you leave enough tips and hints for a newcomer to take over your work in the future.

I wish I had known you were coming (before I quit)

I admit it is not very easy to think about your successors while you are programming. Many times, you just do not realize that your code may end up being taken over by another project, reused by other people or you might eventually be replaced by another person, willing to continue your work thereafter. However, the most remarkable asset of FLOSS is precisely that one: the code will be reused, adapted, integrated or extended by someone else. Maintainability is a critical feature of software engineering. But it becomes paramount in FLOSS. It is not only about source code. It is about people, social relationships and digital etiquette. It is something beyond mere good taste. Quod severis metes ("as you sow, so shall you reap"). Remember that, next time, you may be the newcomer filling the knowledge gap left by a former developer.

Part III.

Mentoring and Recruiting

5. You'll Eventually Know Everything They've Forgotten

Leslie Hawthorn

An internationally known community manager, speaker and author, Leslie Hawthorn has over 10 years experience in high tech project management, marketing and public relations. Recently she joined AppFog as their Community Manager, where she is responsible for developer engagement. Prior to AppFog, she served as Outreach Manager at Oregon State University's Open Source Lab and as a Program Manager for Google's Open Source Team, where she managed the Google Summer of Code Program, created the contest now known as Google Code-in and launched the company's Open Source Developer Blog.

> "The most important documentation for initial users is the basics: how to quickly set up the software, an overview of how it works, perhaps some guides to doing common tasks. Yet these are exactly the things the writers of the documentation know all too well – so well that it can be difficult for them to see things from the reader's point of view, and to laboriously spell out the steps that (to the writers) seem so obvious as to be unworthy of mention." – Karl Fogel, Producing Open Source Software

When you are first starting work on a FOSS project, the learning curve is steep and the path daunting. You may find yourself subscribed to mailing lists or in chat rooms with all kinds of "famous" people, like the creator of your favorite programming language or the maintainer of your favorite package, wondering how you are ever going to be skilled enough to contribute effectively. What you may not realize is how much these wise folk have forgotten along their path to success.

To use a simple simile, the process of learning how to use and develop for any open source project is much like learning to ride a bicycle. For those who are experienced cyclists, "it's as easy as riding a bicycle." You have probably ridden a bike a few times and understand its architecture: saddle, wheels, brakes, pedals and handlebars. Yet you climb aboard, head out on your ride and suddenly discover that riding is not as simplistic as you had thought: at what height should your saddle sit? What gear should you be in when climbing a hill? When descending one? And do you really need that helmet anyway? (Hint: Yes, you do.)

When you first start of cycling, you will not even know what questions to ask and you will only find out by having sore knees, aching lungs and a twinge in your back. Even then, your questions will not always yield the answers you need; someone might know to tell you to lower your saddle when you tell them your knees hurt, but they might also just assume that you are new to this whole thing and eventually you will just figure it out on your own. They have forgotten fighting with gear changes, figuring out that they had the wrong lights and reflectors, and which hand signal indicates a left turn because they have been riding for so long that all these matters are simply second nature to them.

The same scenario holds true when getting started in FOSS. As you are building a package for the first time, you will inevitably run into some obscure error message or other kind of fail. And when you ask for help, some friendly soul will no doubt tell you that "it's easy, just do foo, bar and baz." Except for you, it is not easy, there may be no documentation for foo, bar is not doing what it is supposed to be doing and what is this baz thing anyway with its eight disambiguation entries on Wikipedia? You obviously do not want to be a pest, but you will need help to actually get something done. Perhaps you keep retrying the same steps and keep meeting with fail, getting more and more frustrated. Maybe you wander off, get a coffee and figure you will come back to the problem later. What none of us in the FOSS world want to happen is what happens to many: that cup of coffee is infinitely better than feeling ignorant and intimidated, so you do not try your hand at FOSS any further.

Realize now that you will eventually know those things that the experts around you have forgotten or do not articulate because these steps are obvious to them. Every person more knowledgeable than you went through the same wanderings you are right now when learning how to do the things you are trying to do. Here are a few tips to make your travels easier:

Don't wait too long to ask for help No one wants to be a pest and no one enjoys looking clueless. That being said, if you are unable to fix your problem after trying to do so for 15 minutes, it is time to ask for help. Make sure you check the project's website for documentation so you use the right IRC channel, forum or mailing list for help. Many projects have online communication channels specifically for beginners, so keep an eye out for words like *mentor*, *newbie*, and *getting started*.

Talk about your (thought) process It is not just a matter of asking questions, it is knowing the right questions to ask. When getting started, you will not necessarily know what those questions are, so when asking for help, be detailed about what you are trying to accomplish, the steps you have taken, and the problem you have encountered. Let your would-be mentors in the project IRC channel or on the mailing list know that you have read the manual by including links to the documentation you have read on the topic. If you have not found any documentation, a polite mention of the fact is also helpful.

Know your own value As a new contributor to a project, you are an invaluable asset not for your knowledge, but for your ignorance. When first starting work in FOSS, nothing seems (to you) so obvious as to be unworthy of mention. Take notes on the problems you have encountered and how they were fixed, then use those notes to update the project documentation or work with the community to prepare screen casts or other training materials for particularly tough problems. When you encounter something truly frustrating, realize you are in the spectacular position of helping make sure the next person who comes along does not encounter the same difficulties.

6. University and Community

Kévin Ottens

Kévin Ottens is a long term hacker of the KDE community. He contributed to the KDE Platform at large, with a strong emphasis on API design and frameworks architecture. Graduating in 2007, he holds a PhD in computer science which led him to work particularly on ontologies engineering and multi-agent systems. Kévin's job at KDAB includes developing research projects around KDE technologies. He still lives in Toulouse where he serves as part time teacher in his former university.

Introduction

Free Culture communities are mostly driven by volunteer efforts. Also most of the people getting into such communities do so during their time at the university. It is somewhat the right period of your life to embark in such adventures: you are young, full of energy, curious, and probably want to change the world to your image. That is really all that is needed for most volunteer work.

But, at the same time, being a student does not necessarily leave you plenty of time to engage with a Free Culture community. Indeed, most of these communities are rather large, and it can be frightening to contact them.

It obviously raises a scary question: do Free Culture communities, because they don't try to actively outreach to universities, fail to attract the next generation of talented contributors? That is a valid question we tried to explore in the context of a community producing software, namely KDE. In this article, we focus on the aspects we did not foresee but had to deal with while looking for an answer to this question.

Building relationship with a local university

Really, it all starts by reaching out to the students themselves, and for that, the best way is still to get to their universities, trying to show them how welcoming Free Culture communities can be. To that effect, we built a relationship with the Paul Sabatier University in Toulouse – more precisely one of its courses of study named IUP ISI which focused on software engineering.

The IUP ISI was very oriented toward "hands on" knowledge, and as such had a pre-existing program for student projects. A particularly interesting point of that program is the fact that students work in teams mixing students from different promotions. Third year and fourth year students get to collaborate on a common goal, which usually leads to teams of seven to ten students.

The first year of our experiment we hooked up with that program, proposing new topics for the projects, focusing on software developed within the KDE community. Henri Massié, director of the course of study, has been very welcoming to the idea, and let us put the experiment in place. For that first year, we were allocated two slots for KDE related software projects.

To quickly build trust, we decided that year to provide a few guarantees regarding the work of the students:

- to help the teachers have confidence in the topics covered: the chosen projects were close to the topics taught at the IUP ISI (that is why we targeted a UML modeling tool and a project management tool for that year);

- to give maximum visibility to the teachers: we provided them a server on which the student production was regularly built and remotely accessible for testing purpose;

- to ease the engagement of the students with the community: the maintainers of the projects were appointed to play a "customer" role thus pushing requirements to the students and helping them find their way in the ramifications of the community;

- finally, to get the students going, we introduced a short course on how to develop with Qt and the frameworks produced by KDE;

At the time of this writing, we have been through five years of such projects. Small adjustments to the organization have been done here and there, but most of the ideas behind it stayed the same. Most of the changes made were the result of more and more interest from the community willing to engage with students and of more and more freedom given to us in the topics we could cover in our projects.

Moreover, throughout those years the director gave us continuous support and encouragement, effectively allocating more slots for Free Culture community projects, proving that our integration strategy was right: building trust very quickly is key to a relationship between a Free Culture community and a university.

Realizing teaching is a two-way process

During those years of building bridges between the KDE community and the IUP ISI course of study, we ended up in teaching positions to support the students in their project related tasks. When you have never taught a classroom full of students, you might still have this image of yourself sitting in a classroom a few years ago. Indeed, most teachers were students once... sometimes not even the type of very disciplined or attentive students. You were likely having this feeling of drinking from a firehose: a teacher entering a room, getting in front of the students and delivering knowledge to you.

This stereotype is what most people keep in mind of their years as students and the first time they get in a teaching situation they want to reproduce that stereotype: coming with knowledge to deliver.

The good news is that nothing could be further from the truth than this stereotype. The bad news is that if you try to reproduce it, you are very likely to scare your students away and face nothing else than lack of motivation on their side to engage with the community. The image you give of yourself is the very first thing they will remember of the community: the first time you get in the classroom, to them *you are* the community!

Not falling into the trap of this stereotype requires you to step back a bit and to realize what teaching is really about. It is not a one way process where one delivers knowledge to students. We came to the conclusion that it is instead a two-way process: you get to create a symbiotic relationship with your student. Both the students and the teacher have to leave the classroom with new knowledge. You get to deliver your expertise of course – but to do so efficiently you have to adapt to the students' frame of reference all the time. It is a very humbling work.

Realizing that fact generates quite a few changes in the way you undertake your teaching:

- You will have to understand the culture of your students. They probably have a fairly different background from you and you will have to adapt your discourse to them; for instance, the students we trained are all part of the so-called Y generation which exhibits fairly different traits regarding leadership, loyalty and trust than previous generations.

- You will have to reassess your own expertise, since you will need to adapt your discourse to their culture. You will approach your own knowledge from very different angles than what you are used to, which will inevitably lead you to discoveries in fields you assumed you mastered.

- Finally, you will have to build skills in presenting; a teaching position is really about getting out of your comfort zone to present your own knowledge while keeping it interesting and entertaining to your audience. It will make you a better presenter.

As such, you will become a better teacher. Also your goals of getting well trained students, and having students engage with a Free Culture community will be better fulfilled.

Conclusion

At the end of the day why would you go through all the effort to build trust with a university and step outside of your comfort zone by improving your teaching? Well, it really boils down to the initial question we tried to answer:

Do Free Culture communities fail to attract new contributors out of universities simply because of their inaction?

In our experience the answer is *yes*. Through those five years of building up a relationship with the IUP ISI, we retained around two students per year on average. Some of them disappeared after a while, but some of them become very active contributors. The other ones still keep some nostalgia of that period of their life and keep advocating even though they do not contribute directly. And right now we have a local KDE team which managed to efficiently organize a two day conference for our latest release party.

Of those former students, not a single one would have engaged with KDE without those university projects. We would have completely missed those talents. Luckily, we have not been inactive.

7. Being Allowed to Do Awesome

Lydia Pintscher

Lydia Pintscher is a people geek and cat herder by nature. Among other things, she manages KDE's mentoring programs (Google Summer of Code, Google Code-in, Season of KDE), is a founding member of KDE's Community Working Group and is a board member of KDE e.V.

Free Software has an enemy. It is not who most people on the Internet think it is. No, it is a lack of active participation.

Every single day there are thousands of people out there looking for a way to put meaning into their life, looking for ways to do something that truly matters. Every single day thousands of lines of code for Free Software projects are waiting to be written and debugged, programs are waiting to be promoted and translated, artwork is waiting to be created and much more. Sadly, far too often the people fail to connect with projects. There are several reasons for that. It starts with people not knowing about Free Software at all and its benefits and purpose. But we are getting there. People are starting to use and maybe even understand Free Software on a large scale. Free Software projects live by converting some of those users into active contributors. This is where the problems begin.

I have managed hundreds of students in mentoring programs and have been doing outreach in various forms for Free Software projects. I've worked with enthusiastic people whose life was changed for the better by their contributions to Free Software. But there is one theme I see over and over again and it breaks my heart because I now know what talent we are missing out on: not being allowed to do awesome. It is best summarized by what a fellow Google Summer of Code mentor said: "The insight that most people in Open Source didn't get allowed to work on stuff but just didn't run fast enough at the right moment seems to be rare". Potential contributors often think they are not allowed to contribute. The reasons for this are many and they are all misconceptions. The most common misconceptions in my experience are:

- "I can not write code. There can not possibly be a way for me to contribute."
- "I am not really good at this. My help is not needed."
- "I would just be a burden. They have more important things to worry about."
- "I am not needed. They must already have enough much more brilliant people than me."

Those are almost always false and I wish I had known a long time ago that they are so prevalent. I would have done a lot of my initial outreach efforts differently.

The easiest way of getting someone out of this situation is to invite them personally. "That workshop we are doing? Oh yes, you should come." "That bug in the bug tracker? I'm sure you're the perfect person to try to fix it." "That press release we need to get done? It would be great if you could read over it and make sure it is good." And if that is not possible, make sure that your outreach material (you have some, right?) clearly states what kind of people you are looking for and what you consider the basic requirements. Make sure to especially reach out to people outside your usual contributor base because for them this barrier is even bigger. And unless you overcome that, you will only recruit who you are – meaning you will get more contributors just like the ones you already have. People like the people you already have are great, but think about all the other great people you are missing out on, who could bring new ideas and skills to your project.

Part IV.

Infrastructure

8. Love the Unknown

Jeff Mitchell

Jeff Mitchell spends his working days dabbling in all sorts of computer and networking technologies, his off-time dabbling in all sorts of FOSS projects and most enjoys a confluence of both. After serving as a system administrator in a professional capacity between 1999-2005, he has since kept his skills sharp by performing volunteer work for various workplace and FOSS projects. These days, most of his FOSS time is spent as a sysadmin for KDE and a core developer of Tomahawk Player. Jeff currently lives in Boston, USA.

Recently I was part of a group interviewing a potential new sysadmin at work. We had gone through a few dozen resumes and had finally brought our first candidate in for an interview. The candidate – let's call him John – had experience with smaller, lab-style computer clusters as well as larger data center operations. At first, things were proceeding apace, except that he had an odd answer to a few of our questions: "I'm a sysadmin." The meaning of that statement was not immediately clear to us, until the following exchange occurred:

> **Me**: So you've said that you don't have Cisco IOS experience, but what about networking in general?
> **John**: Well, I'm a sysadmin.
> **Me**: Right, but – how about networking concepts? Routing protocols like BGP or OSPF, VLANs, bridges ...
> **John, exasperated**: I'm a *sysadmin.*

That was when we understood what he was saying. John had not been telling us that he knew of the various things we were asking about because he was a sysadmin; he was telling us that because he was a sysadmin he did *not* know about those things. John was a *systems* administrator; claiming such was his hand-waving way of indicating that those tasks belonged to network administrators. Probably unsurprisingly, John did not get the job.

For many open source projects, specialization is a curse, not a blessing. Whether a project falls into one category or the other often depends on the size of the development team; specialization to the degree of single points of failure can mean serious disruption to a project in the event of a developer leaving, whether on good, bad or unfortunate terms. It is no different for open source project sysadmins, although the general scarcity of these seems to allow projects to adopt sometimes dangerous tolerances.

The most egregious example I have seen involved one particular project whose documentation site (including all of their installation and configuration documentation) was down for over a month. The reason: the server had crashed, and the only person with access to that server was sailing around on a "pirate ship" with members of Sweden's Pirate Party. That really happened.

However, not all single points of failure are due to absentee system administrators; some are artificial. One large project's system administration access rights decisions were handled by a single lead administrator, who not only reserved some access rights solely for himself (you guessed it: yes, he did disappear for a while and yes, that did cause problems) but made decisions about how access rights should be given out based on whether he himself trusted the candidate. "Trust" in this case was based on one thing; it was not based on how many community members vouched for that person, how long that person had been an active and trusted contributor to that project, or even how long he had known that individual as a part of that project. Rather, it was based on how well he personally knew someone, by which he meant how well he knew that individual *in person*. Imagine how well that scales to a distributed global team of system administrators.

Of course, this example only goes to show that it is very difficult for open source sysadmins to walk the line between security and capability. Large corporations can afford redundant staff, even when those staff are segmented into different responsibilities or security domains. Redundancy is important, but what if the only current option for redundant system administration is taking the first guy that randomly pops into your IRC channel and volunteers to help? How can you reasonably trust that person, their skills, or their motives? Unfortunately, only the project's contributors, or some subset of them, can determine when the right person has come along, using the same Web of Trust model that underpins much of the rest of the open source world. The universe of open source projects, their needs, and those willing to contribute to any particular project is blissfully diverse; as a result, human dynamics, trust, intuition and how to apply these concepts to any particular open source project are broad topics that are far out of scope of this short essay.

One key thing has made walking that security/capability line far easier, however: the rise of distributed version control systems, or DVCSes. In the past, access control was paramount because the heart of any open source project – its source code – was centralized. I realize that many out there will now be thinking "Jeff, you should know better than that; the heart of a project is its community, not its code!" My response is simple: community members come and go, but if someone accidentally runs "rm -rf" on the entire centralized VCS tree of your project and you lack backups, how many of those community members are going to be willing to stick around and help recreate everything from scratch? (This is actually based on a real example, where a drunk community member angry at some code he was debugging ran an "rm -rf" on his entire checkout, *intending* to destroy all code in the project. Fortunately, he was not a sysadmin with access to the central repository, and too drunk to remember his copy was simply a checkout.)

A project's code is its heart; its community members are its lifeblood. Without either, you are going to have a hard time keeping a project alive. With a centralized VCS, if you did not have the foresight to set up regular backups, maybe you could get lucky and be able to cobble together the entire source tree from checkouts that different people had of different parts of the tree, but for most projects the history of the code is as important as the current code itself, and you will still have lost all of it.

That is no longer the case. When every local clone has all of the history for a project and nightly backups can be performed by having a cron job run something as simple as "git pull", the centralized repository is now just a coordination tool. This takes its status down a few notches. It still has to be protected against threats both internal and external: unpatched systems are still vulnerable to known exploits, a malicious sysadmin can still wreak havoc, an ineffective authentication system can allow malicious code into your codebase, and an accidental "rm -rf" of the centralized repository can still cause loss of developer time. But these challenges can be overcome, and in the day and age of cheap VPS and data center hosting, absentee sysadmins can be overcome too. (Better make sure you have redundant access to DNS, though! Oh, and, put your websites in a DVCS repository too, and make branches for local modifications. You will thank me later.) So, DVCSes give your project redundant hearts nearly for free, which is a great way to help open source sysadmins sleep at night and makes us all feel a little bit more like Time Lords. It also means if you are not on a DVCS, stop reading this very moment and go switch to one. It is not just about workflows and tools. If you care about the safety of your code and your project, you will switch.

Source code redundancy is a must, and in general the greater amount of redundancy you can manage, the more robust your systems. It may also seem obvious that you want sysadmin redundancy; what you may not find obvious is that redundant sysadmins are not as important as redundant skillsets. John, the systems administrator, worked in data centers and companies with redundant sysadmins but rigid, defined skillsets. While that worked for large companies that could pay to acquire new sysadmins with particular skillsets on-demand, most open source projects do not have that luxury. You have to make do with what you can get. This of course means that an alternative (and sometimes the only alternative) to finding redundant system administrators is spreading the load, having other project members each pick up a skill or two until redundancy is achieved.

It is really no different from the developer or artwork side of a project; if half of your application is written in C++ and half is written in Python, and only one developer knows Python, a departure from the project by that developer will cause massive short-term problems and could cause serious long-term problems as well. Encouraging developers to branch out and become familiar with more languages, paradigms, libraries, and so on means that each of your developers becomes more valuable, which should not come as a shock; acquiring new skillsets is a byproduct of further education, and more educated personnel are more valuable. (This also makes their CV more valuable, which should provide a good driving force.)

Most open source developers that I know find it a challenge and a pleasure to keep testing new waters, as that is the behavior that led them to open source development in the first place. Similarly, open source system administrators are in scarce supply, and can not afford to get stuck in a rut. New technologies relevant to the sysadmin are always emerging, and there are often ways to use existing or older technologies in novel ways to enhance infrastructure or improve efficiency.

John was not a good candidate because he brought little value; he brought little value because he had never pushed outside of his defined role. Open source sysadmins falling into that trap do not just hurt the project they are currently involved with, they reduce their value to other projects using different infrastructure technologies that could desperately use a hand; this decreases the overall capability of the open source community. To the successful open source administrator, there is no such thing as a comfort zone.

9. Backups to Maintain Sanity

Austin Appel

Austin "scorche" Appel is an information security professional who spends his time breaking into things previously thought secure (with permission, of course). He is often seen around security/hacker conferences teaching people how to pick locks. In the open source world, he does a host of things for the Rockbox project and previously volunteered for the One Laptop Per Child project.

Backups are good. Backups are great. A competent admin always keeps current backups. This much can be gathered from any manual on server administration. The problem is that backups are only really used when absolutely necessary. If something drastic happens to the server or its data and one is forced to fall back on something, the backups will come to the rescue in the moment of most dire need. However, this should never happen, right? At any other time, what does having backups do for you and your server environment?

Before going further, it is important to note that the advice espoused is for the smaller open source project server administrators out there – the silent majority. If you maintain services that would cause a large amount of frustration, and even perhaps harm if they experienced any downtime, please take this with a very small grain of salt.

For the rest of us who work with countless smaller projects with limited resources, we rarely have a separate test and production server. In fact, with all of the many services that an open source project typically needs to maintain (version control, web services, mailing lists, forums, build bots, databases, bug/feature trackers, etc.), separate testing environments are often the stuff we can only dream about. Unfortunately, the typical approach to system administration is to tread lightly and only upgrade the systems when absolutely necessary, to avoid risking dependency issues, broken code, or any of the other million things that could go wrong. The reason you are nervous is not because you may be inexperienced. It is important to know that you are not alone in this. Whether or not we admit it to others, many of us have been (and likely still are) in this position. The sad fact is that this inaction – stemming from the fear of breaking a "working" system – often leads to running services which are often several versions behind the curve, and come with a host of potentially serious security vulnerabilities. Rest assured that this is not the only way to play the game though.

People tend to play a game differently when they have infinite lives as compared to needing to start over from the start as soon as one mistake is made. Why should server administration be any different? Approaching the concept of backups with an offensive mindset can change your whole view of administrating systems. Instead of living in fear from a complete dist-upgrade (or equivalent command for yum, pacman, etc.), when armed with backups, one is free to update the packages on a server secure in the knowledge that the changes can always be rolled back if things turn sour. The key to getting over this is all about a state-of-mind. There is no reason to fear as long as you have your safety net of backed-up files beneath you as you jump. After all, system administration is constantly a learning experience.

Of course, if you do not validate your backups, relying on backups in this way becomes a very dangerous game. Fortunately, experienced system administrators know that the commandment "keep current backups" is always followed by "validate your backups." Again, this is another mantra that people like to recite. What does not fit as elegantly into a catchy mantra is how quickly and easily validating backups can be accomplished. The best way to tell that a backup works is, of course, to restore it (preferably on an identical system not currently active). But again, in the absence of such luxuries, a bit more creativity is required. This is where (at least for files) checksums can help you determine the integrity of your backed-up files. In rsync, for example, the default method it uses to determine which files have been modified is to check the time of last modification and size of the file. However, by using the "-c" option, rsync will use a 128-bit MD4 checksum to determine whether files have changed or not. While this may not always be the best idea to do every time in all situations due to likely taking much longer than a normal rsync and increased io usage, this ensures that the files are intact.

The role of system administrator can be a stressful one at times. However, there is no need to make it more so than it needs to be. With the proper frame of mind, some ostensibly single-purpose defense-seeming tasks can be used as valuable tools to allow you to nimbly move forward with your sanity intact with the speed appreciated by all open source projects.

Part V.

Code

10. The Art of Problem Solving

Thiago Macieira

Thiago Macieira holds a double degree in Engineering and an MBA, but his involvement in Open Source predates those, getting close to 15 years now. An active participant in the KDE, Qt and MeeGo communities, he's been a software engineer and product manager for Qt, giving presentations and listening to people. These days, Thiago lives in Oslo, Norway and when he's not working on Qt, he tries (with limited success) to improve his skills at StarCraft 2.

Problems are a routine we are faced with almost every day of our lives and solving them is so recurrent we often do not realize we are doing it. They may be situations as simple as figuring out the best path to get to a destination or how to set the items in the fridge so they fit. Only when we fail to solve them immediately do we take notice, since we have to stop and think about them. The professional life is no different and solving professional problems becomes part of the job description.

Problem solving was the topic of my inaugural class when I started my engineering degree. In that overcrowded amphitheatre last century, our professor explained to roughly 700 freshmen how engineers are problem solvers and our professional lives would be moving from one problem to be solved to another. Some problems would be small and we would solve them in no time; some others would be so big we would need to have a project setting and a team to crack, most would fall in-between. He then proceeded to give examples on how the mentality of "problem solver" helped him in his professional and personal life, including one unexpected live example when the projector failed on us.

The ability to solve problems is a skill we can hone with practice and some ground work. Practice is something one must acquire only through experience, by trial and failure, therefore it is not something that a book could teach. Getting started in solving problems, however, is something one can learn. If experience is the toolbox we carry when facing new issues, the techniques of problem solving are the instructions on how to use the tools in the toolbox.

Phrasing the question correctly

The question we are trying to answer is the direction we are going to go when trying to solve the problem. Ask the wrong question and the answers may be irrelevant, invalid or just plainly wrong. Consequently, asking the correct question is paramount. Moreover, asking the correct question correctly is important, since it provides clues as to what we are seeking.

The most useless problem statement that one can face is "it doesn't work", yet we seem to get it far too often. It is a true statement, as evidently something is off. Nevertheless, the phrasing does not provide any clue as to where to start looking for answers.

Bug-tracking systems often request that the bug reporter describe the actions taken that led up to the problem being seen, the description of what happened (that is, the symptom) and a description of what was expected to happen. The comparison between the symptom and the expected behavior is a good source for the question to be asked: why did this happen, why did this other behavior not happen? While this is not the only way for creating the question, applying this technique to problems may certainly help.

Phrasing the problem and the question correctly, in all its details, is also a way to further describe the problem statement. First, we must realize that the problem very likely does not lie where we are expecting it to be – if it did, we would have probably solved the problem by now. Explaining all the details of the problem at hand provides the help-givers with more information to work with. In addition, even if counter-intuitively, the act of describing the problem in its entirety often leads to finding of the solution, so much so that many development groups require "stuck" developers to perform this task, either by discussing it with a colleague or talking to a "naïve" entity, like a rubber duck or Mr. Potato-Head.

In addition, one must return to the question every now and then, so as to not lose sight of what the goal is. While executing activities to solve the problem, care must be taken not to concentrate exclusively on a particular piece of the problem, forgetting the overall objective. For the same reason, it is necessary to re-examine the initial question when a possible solution is found, to ensure it does solve the entire problem. In turn, this also shows the necessity of asking the right question, stating the complete problem: without the full question, the solution may be equally incomplete.

Divide et conquera

Experience in helping others trying to solve their problems online has shown me that in general people treat their issues as monolithic, indivisible stumbling blocks that must be dealt with as a whole. As such, a large problem poses a very difficult question to be answered in its entirety.

In truth, the vast majority of those issues can be further broken down into smaller problems, each of which are easier to deal with and determine if they are the root cause of the problem, not to mention the possibility of there being multiple sources for the symptom experienced. Repeating this operation just a couple of times will yield much smaller problems to tackle and, therefore, quicker solutions. However, the more divisions we are forced to make, the more we are required to know about the operating internals of the system at hand. In reality, the problem solver will only break down as far as his knowledge of the subject will permit and then work on the issue from there.

For software development, the subsystems being used are often good hints at where to break up the problem. For example, if the problem involves a TCP/IP transmission of data, two possible divisions are the sender and the receiver: it is of no use to look for the problem on the receiver's end if the sender is not transmitting the data properly. Similarly, a graphical application that is not showing the data that it is fetching from a database has a clear division: it would be a good idea to verify that the database access works before investigating why it is not displayed properly. Alternatively, one could feed dummy data to the display functions and then verify that said data does get displayed properly.

Even when the groupings are not clear, dividing the problem can still help shed light on the issue. In fact, almost every division is helpful, as it reduces the amount of code to be inspected, and with it the complexity to be dealt with. At an extreme, simply dividing the code in two and searching for the problem in one half may be of use. This technique, called bisecting, is recommended if the divisions created from the subsystems and interfaces have not yet revealed a solution.

The end-product of a sequence of proper divisions is a small, self-contained example showing the problem. At this stage, one of three options is usually right: the problem can be identified and located; the code is actually correct and the expectations were wrong; or a bug was found on the lower layer of code. An advantage of the process is that it also produces a test-case to be sent in a bug report, should a bug turn out to be the cause.

Boundary conditions

An issue similar to dividing the problem is that of the boundary conditions. In mathematics and physics, boundary conditions are the set of values for the variables that determine the region of validity of the equations being solved. For software, boundary conditions are the set of conditions that must be met for the code to perform properly. Usually, the boundary conditions are far from simple: unlike mathematics and physics, the variables in software systems are far too many, which means that the boundary conditions for them are equally many.

In software systems, the boundary conditions are often referred to as "preconditions", which are conditions that must be met before a certain action is allowed. Verifying that the preconditions have been met is good exercise in the searching for an answer, for a violation of the preconditions is definitely a problem that needs solving – even if it is not the root cause of the original problem. Examples of preconditions can be as simple as the fact that a pointer must be valid before it can be dereferenced or that an object must not have been disposed of before it can be used. Complex preconditions are very likely to be documented for the software being used.

Another interesting group of boundary conditions is characterized, interestingly, by what is not permitted: the undefined behavior. This type of boundary conditions is very common when dealing with specifications, which try to be very explicit in how software should behave. A good example of this are the compilers and language definitions. Strictly speaking, dereferencing a null pointer is an undefined behavior: the most common consequence is a processor exception being trapped and the program terminating, but other behaviors are permitted too, including working perfectly.

The right tool for the right job

If engineers are problem-solvers, the engineer's motto is "use the right tool for the right job". It may seem obvious, as no one is expected to use a hammer to solve an electronic problem. Nonetheless, cases of using the wrong tool are quite common, often due to ignorance of the existence of a better tool.

Some of these tools are the bread-and-butter of software development, like the compiler and the debugger. Inability to use these tools are unforgivable: the professional who finds himself in an environment with new or unknown tools, such as when switching positions or jobs, must dedicate some time to learning them, becoming familiar with their functionalities and limitations. For example, if a program crashes, being able to determine the location of the crash as well as variables being accessed in that section of the code may help determine the root cause and thus point to the solution.

Some other tools are more advanced, belong to a niche, are not very widely known, or are available only under cost or conditions which cannot be met by the engineer. Yet they can be incredibly useful in helping elucidate problems. Such tools may be static code checker tools, thread checkers, memory debuggers, hardware event loggers, etc. For instance, development hardware often contains a way to control it via a special interface like JTAG or dump all instructions executed and processor state, but this requires having special hardware and tools, which are not readily available and usually cost more than volume, consumer devices. A different example is the valgrind suite of tools, which include thread checkers and memory debuggers and is readily available for free, but are part of the advanced, niche tools and are not taught at schools.

Knowing the contents of one's toolbox is a powerful knowledge. Using a specialized tool to search for a problem will likely yield a result quicker, be it positive, confirming the problem, or negative, which in turn leads the search elsewhere. Moreover, it is important to know how to use these tools, which justifies spending time reading the documentation, in training or simply experimenting with them with known problems to understand how to proceed.

Conclusion

Solving problems is an art available to all. Like other arts, some people may have such a skill that it may seem that they were born with the ability. But in reality, with enough experience and practice, solving problems becomes an unconscious activity.

When faced with a problem that is not easy to solve, one should sit back and take a clear look at the entirety of the problem. What is the problem we have? Can we phrase the question that we need an answer for? Once we know what we are looking for, we can start searching for where it may be located. Can we break it down into smaller, more manageable pieces? What are the best tools to be used for each piece? Have we verified that we are using the functionalities and services correctly?

After solving many problems, we start to see patterns. It will become easier to detect subtle hints from the symptoms and direct the searching towards the actual problem. An experienced problem-solver may not even realize this action is taking place. That is an indication that the experience and behavior has set in so well that no conscious effort is required to access those skills.

Yet there are always some problems in life that will be hard to solve, ranging from professional, existential, philosophical or for pure curiosity. Then again, it is the challenge that drives us, the need to understand more. Life would be pretty tedious otherwise.

11. Cross-Project Collaboration

Henri Bergius

Henri Bergius is the founder of Midgard, a free software content repository. He has also been involved for a long time in making Linux desktops location-aware, and in the Maemo and MeeGo communities. He runs a small consultancy called Nemein, hacks in CoffeeScript and PHP, and spends much of his free time motorcycling through remote parts of the Eurasian continent. He lives in the cold Nordic city of Helsinki, Finland.

> There may be a whole new system where you're defined more and more by who you are and not by what you own, by what you've created and shared, and what other people have then built on" – Former Xerox PARC director John Seely Brown in An Optimist's Tour of the Future (Mark Stevenson, 2010)

On projects and communities

Much of the free software world is split into tribes gathered around something called projects. There are major projects like GNOME, KDE or Drupal, and lots of smaller projects revolving around a single application or a library.

Actually, calling them projects is kind of silly.

In my mind, a project is a plan of effort towards an achievable aim, with a schedule that has start and end dates. So, for example GNOME 3.1 would be a project, but GNOME as whole is not. It is a community of individuals maintaining and creating a body of software through various smaller efforts, or projects.

Enough with pedantry. The problem with the concept of projects is that they end up keeping people apart, creating insular communities that often are reluctant or unable to collaborate with "the competition". But in the end, all of these communities consist of individuals who write free software, and it is their choice whether this software can be used in different environments or not.

In the end we all want the software we created to be used by others. And even better, we want others to join in our efforts and build cool stuff on what we have created. That is, after all, what is in the heart of free software.

So why do we enact these walls around ourselves? Keeping an insulated community just fosters an us-versus-them mentality. The incompatibilities of different programming languages already do so much to keep us apart, why add to that?

The Midgard lesson

What I wish I had known when I started, in those optimistic dot-com days of the late 90s, is that in reality software efforts do not need to be isolated. With a bit of care we can share our software and ideas across communities, making both the communities and our software stronger and better.

When I started my free software career, it was a time of big projects. Netscape was open-sourced, the Apache Software Foundation was getting a form, and venture-funded efforts were going on everywhere. It felt like a norm to try and build your own community. This was the sure path to fame, fortune and building cool stuff.

So what we did was build our own web framework. Back then there were not that many of them, especially for the fledgling PHP language. PHP was not even the first choice for us, only picked after a long debate about using Scheme which our lead developer preferred. But PHP was gaining popularity, becoming the programming language of the web. And web was what we wanted to build.

At first, things looked very promising. Lots of developers flocked into our community and started contributing. There were even companies founded around Midgard. And the framework became more featureful, and more tighly coupled.

In hindsight, this was the mistake we made. We positioned Midgard to be something apart from PHP itself. Something that you would install separately, and build whole websites on top of. It was either our way or the highway.

With Midgard you would have to use our content repository interfaces for everything, as well as our user management and permissions model. You would have to use our templating system, and store much of your code into the repository instead of a file system.

This obviously did not sit too well with the wider PHP community. Our ideas were strange to them, and Midgard at the time was even distributed as a huge patch to the codebase, as PHP3 did not have loadable modules.

Many years have passed, and PHP's popularity has waxed and waned. At the same time the Midgard community has been quite constant – a small, tightly knit group making progress in the long run, but apart from the wider PHP world.

We always wondered why we found it so hard to interact with the PHP world. Even some communities doing something completely different, like the GNOME desktop, secmed easier to approach. Only recently, after years of isolation, we realized the problem. In a nutshell: frameworks keep us apart, while libraries allow us to share our code and experiences.

On libraries and frameworks

In the end, software is about automation, about building tools that people can use for solving problems or connecting with each other. With software, these tools have many layers in them. There are low-level services like an operating system, then there are libraries, frameworks and toolkits, and then there are actual applications.

Applications are always written for some particular usecase, and so between them there are very few opportunities for sharing code.

The much more appealing opportunity is on the libraries and frameworks level. A framework, if generic enough, can usually be utilized for building different sorts of software. And a library can be used to bring a particular piece of logic or connectivity anywhere. In my view, this is the layer where most programming should happen, with specific applications being just something that connects various libraries into a framework that then runs the actual app.

What is a library and what is a framework? People often use these terms interchangeably, but there is a useful rule of thumb to know which is which: a library is something that your code calls, while a framework is something that calls your code.

If you want your code to be used and improved upon, the best way to go about it is to maximize the number of potential users and contributors. With free software, this works by ensuring your code can be adapted to multiple different situations and environments.

In the end, what you want to do is to build a library. Libraries are cool.

How to make collaboration work

The hardest part is to get over the barrier of them-versus-us. The developers of the other community are hackers building free software, just like you. So just get over the question and start talking with them.

After you have the discussion going, here are some points that I have found important when actually implementing common ideas or libraries across project boundaries:

- Use permissive licensing and try to avoid copyright assignments or other requirements potential users would find onerous.

- Host the project on neutral ground. For web projects, Apache is quite a good home. For desktop projects, Freedesktop is probably the best option.

- Use technologies that do not impose too many constraints. Libraries should be quite low-level, or provide D-Bus APIs that can be used with any system.

- Avoid framework-specific dependencies. For example, KDE has found GeoClue hard to adopt because it uses GNOME-specific settings interfaces.

- Meet the other guys. If you are from the GNOME project, go to aKademy and give a talk, and if you are a KDE developer, go and talk at GUADEC. After you have shared a beer or two collaboration over IRC happens much more naturally.

- Finally, accept that not everybody will use your implementation. But if they at least implement the same ideas, then collaboration is still possible.

Good luck with breaking down the project boundaries! In most cases it works if your ideas are good and presented with an open mind. But even if you do not find a common ground, as long as your implementation solves the use case for you it has not been in vain. After all, delivering software, and delivering great user experience is what counts.

12. Writing Patches

Kai Blin

Kai Blin is a computational biologist searching for antibiotics in his day job, both at the computer and in the lab. He feels very happy that he gets to release the software developed at work under Open Source licenses. Living in the lovely southern German town of Tübingen, Kai spends some of his evenings at the computer, programming for the Samba project. Most of his remaining spare time is spent at the theatre, where Kai is active both on stage as well as building props, stage and handling other techie things backstage.

Writing patches and submitting them often is the first real interaction you can have with an Open Source project. They are the first impression you give to the developers there. Getting your first patches "right", however that is judged by the particular project you are contributing to, will make your life much easier.

The exact rules on what the patch should look like, how you need to send it to the project and all the other details will probably vary with every project you want to contribute to. I have found that few general rules hold pretty much all the time, and that is what this essay is about.

How to get things wrong

This book is about "things we wish we had known when we got started", so let me get started with the story of my first patches. I first got involved in real coding during the Google Summer of Code™ 2005. The Wine project had accepted me to implement

NTLM crypto based on some Samba-related tool. Wine is a single-committer project, meaning that only the lead developer, Alexandre Julliard, has commit access to the main repository. Back in 2005, Wine still was using CVS as its version control. When the project started and I got the email that I was accepted, I got hold of my mentor on IRC and got to work.

Coding away happily, I got the first features implemented. I produced a patch for my mentor to review. In the olden CVS days, you had to provide all the diff options manually, but I had read up on that part. `cvs diff -N -u > ntlm.patch` and I had the file I could send to my mentor. Actually this is one thing I did get right, and the first thing you should consider when you prepare a patch. The normal output from the diff command might be easier to read for a computer, but I never met a human who actually preferred the normal output over the unified diff output. Switched on by the `-u` flag, this makes diff use the $+++$ and $---$ notation.

For example, the following diff is the result of teaching the Python "Hello, world!" example program to greet the world in Swedish.

```
diff --git a/hello.py b/hello.py
index 59dbef8..6334aa2 100644
--- a/hello.py
+++ b/hello.py
@@ -1,4 +1,4 @@
 #!/usr/bin/env python
 # vim: set fileencoding=utf-8

-print "Hello, world!"
+print "Hallå, världen!"
```

The line starting with `-` is the line being removed, the one starting with `+` is the one being added. The other lines are helping the `patch` tool to do it's job.

My newly created unified diff was sent to my mentor, who gave me a review and lots of things I could change. I fixed that stuff, and sent him a new diff shortly after. The code–review cycle continued for the whole duration of GSoC, with my patch growing and growing. When the pencils down date arrived, I had a huge monster patch with all my changes in there. Naturally I had a really hard time getting that patch reviewed, let alone committed. In the end, Alexandre refused to look at the patch further before I split it up. Wine policy requires that patches are small logical steps adding functionality. Each patch needs to do something useful *and* compile.

Now, splitting an existing huge patch up in pieces that individually make sense *and* compile is a lot of work. It was even more work because the only way I knew this could be done was to write a small patch, create the diff, get that committed, update my local checkout and then write the next small patch. Shortly after I started sending my first small patches, Wine went into a one month feature freeze leading up to the 0.9.0 beta release. I was sitting on my next patch for a month before I could continue, and I eventually got my last patch in in November. I was totally frustrated with the whole experience and decided I did not want to deal with the Wine community anymore.

My frustration held up until people who were actually using my code were starting to ask questions about it in February 2006. My code was actually useful! They wanted more features as well. When Google went on to announce it would be doing GSoC again in 2006, my plans for the summer were clear. Now that Wine had switched to git in December 2005, I knew I would not be held up by possible code freezes, as I finally could create all my small patches locally. Life was good.

It wasn't until I stumbled over a git frontend (called porcelain in git-speak) that emulated the "quilt" behavior that I learned that there were tools that could have made my life easier even in 2005.

How NOT to get things wrong

After my tale of how I managed to get things wrong with regard to sending patches, let me continue with a few tips to avoid the pitfalls.

Patch submission guidelines

The first tip I have is to read up on any patch submission guidelines the project you want to contribute to might have. Those should actually be consulted before you start coding, along with any coding style guidelines the project has.

Unified diffs

Even if not covered in the patch submission guidelines explicitly, you really, really want to send unified diff output. I have yet to meet a project that prefers the non-unified output of diff. Unified diffs make reviewing the patch so much easier. It is no accident that most modern version control programs automatically use that format in their diff command.

Use distributed version control

Speaking of modern version control, you will want to use a DVCS to work on the code locally. Git or Mercurial are the most popular choices there, Bazaar might be worth a look as well. Even if the project you want to contribute to still uses a centralized version control, being able to commit your changes iteratively is a great thing. All of the mentioned distributed version control tools should be able to import commits from SVN or CVS. You could go and learn quilt, but seriously, the future is in the field of distributed version control.

Small patches, doing one thing at a time

When I have to review patches, patches that are too big or that try to do many things at once are really annoying to deal with. Patches doing only one thing at a time are easier to review. Eventually, they will make your life easier when you finally need to debug the mistakes both the author and the reviewer of the patch missed.

Track your patch

After you have submitted your patch, keep an eye on the communication channels of the project and on your patch. If you have not gotten any feedback for a week, you should politely ask for feedback. Depending how the project handles patch submissions, a patch might get lost in the noise. Do not expect to get your patch committed in the first iteration. It usually takes a couple of tries to get used to the style of a new project. As a first-time contributor, nobody will blame you for this, provided you get most of the things right. Just make sure that you fix all of the things the developers indicated and send a second version of the patch.

Conclusion

Writing good patches is not hard. There are a couple of things to consider, but after writing a couple of them you should be on top of those. A modern (distributed) version control system and the workflow you get using it actually take care of most of the things I mentioned.

If you remember nothing else, remember this...

- Use a distributed version control system to manage your patches
- Write patches changing code in small, self-contained steps
- Follow the existing coding conventions
- Respond to comments on your patch promptly

The above guidelines should help you to do most if not all things right when submitting your first patches. Happy coding.

Part VI.

Quality Assurance

13. Given Enough Eyeballs, Not All Bugs are Shallow

Ara Pulido

Ara Pulido is a testing engineer working for Canonical, first as part of the Ubuntu QA team, and now as part of the Hardware Certification team. Although she started her career as a developer, she quickly found out that what she really liked was testing the software. She is very interested in new testing techniques and tries to apply her knowledge to make Ubuntu better.

Dogfooding Is Not Enough

I have been involved with Free Software since my early days at university in Granada. There, with some friends, we founded the local Linux User Group and organized several activities to promote Free Software. But, since I left university, and until I started working at Canonical, my professional career had been in the proprietary software industry, first as a developer and after that as a tester.

When working in a proprietary software project, testing resources are very limited. A small testing team continues the work that developers started with unit testing, using their expertise to find as many bugs as possible, to release the product in good shape for end user consumption. In the Free Software world, however, everything changes.

When I was hired at Canonical, apart from fulfilling the dream of having a paid job in a Free Software project, I was amazed by the possibilities that testing a Free Software project brought. The development of the product happens in the open, and users can access the software in the early stages, test it and file bugs as they encounter them. For a person passionate about testing, this is a new world with lots of new possibilities. I wanted to make the most of it.

As many people do, I thought that dogfooding, or using the software that you are aiming to release, was the most important testing activity that we could do in Free Software. But, if "given enough eyeballs all the bugs are shallow", (one of the key lessons of Raymond's "The Cathedral & The Bazaar"), and Ubuntu had millions of users, why were very important bugs still slipping into the release?

First thing that I found when I started working at Canonical was that the organized testing activities were very few or nonexistent. The only testing activities that were somehow organized were in the form of emails sent to a particular mailing list calling for testing a package in the development version of Ubuntu. I do not believe that this can be considered a proper testing activity, but just another form of dogfooding. This kind of testing generates a lot of duplicated bugs, as a really easy to spot bug will be filed by hundreds of people. Unfortunately, the really hard to spot but potentially critical bug, if someone files it, is likely to remain unnoticed, due to the noise created by the other hundreds of bugs.

Looking better

Is this situation improving? Are we getting better at testing in Free Software projects? Yes, I really believe so.

During the latest Ubuntu development cycles we have started several organized testing activities. The range of topics for these activities is wide, including areas like new desktop features, regression testing, X.org drivers testing or laptop hardware testing. The results of these activities are always tracked, and they prove to be really useful for developers, as they are able to know if the new features are working correctly, instead of guessing that they work correctly because of the absence of bugs.

Regarding tools that help testing, many improvements have been made:

- Apport[1] has contributed to increase the level of detail of the bugs reported against Ubuntu: crashers include all the debugging information and their duplicates are found and marked as such; people can report bugs based on symptoms, etc.

- Launchpad[2], with its upstream connections, has allowed having a full view of the bugs, knowing that bugs happening in Ubuntu are usually bugs in the upstream projects, and allowing developers to know if the bugs are being solved there.

- Firefox, with its Test Pilot extension and program, drives the testing without having to leave the browser[3]. This is, I believe, a much better way to reach testers than a mailing list or an IRC channel.

- The Ubuntu QA team is testing the desktop in an automated fashion and reporting results every week[4], allowing developers to have a very quick way to check that there have not been any major regressions during the development.

Although testing in Free Software projects is getting better, there is still a lot to be done.

Looking ahead

Testing is a skilled activity that requires lots of expertise, but in the Free Software community is still seen as an activity that does not require much effort. One of the reasons could be that the way we do testing is still very old-fashioned and does not reflect the increase

[1] http://wiki.ubuntu.com/Apport
[2] http://launchpad.net
[3] http://testpilot.mozillalabs.com
[4] http://reports.qa.ubuntu.com/reports/desktop-testing/natty

of complexity in the Free Software world in the last decade. How can it be possible that with the amount of innovation that we are generating in Free Software communities, testing is still done like it was in the 80s? Let's face it, fixed testcases are boring and get easily outdated. How are we going to grow a testing community, who is supposed to find meaningful bugs if their main required activity is updating testcases?

But, how do we improve testing? Of course, we cannot completely get rid of testcases, but we need to change the way we create and maintain them. Our testers and users are intelligent, so, why creating step-by-step scripts? Those could easily get replaced by an automated testing tool. Instead of that, let's just have a list of activities you perform with the application and some properties it should have, for example, "Shortcuts in the launcher can be rearranged" or "Starting up LibreOffice is fast". Testers will figure out how to do it, and will create their testcases as they test.

But this is not enough, we need better tools to help testers know what to test, when and how. What about having an API to allow developers to send messages to testers about updates or new features that need testing? What about an application that tell us what part of our system needs testing based on testing activity? In the case of Ubuntu we have the data in Launchpad (we would need testing data as well, but at least we have bug data). If I want to start a testing session against a particular component I would love to have the areas that have not been tested yet and a list of the five bugs with more duplicates for that particular version, so I avoid filing those again. I would love to have all this information without leaving the same desktop that I am testing. This is something that Firefox has started with Test Pilot, although they are currently mainly gathering browser activity.

Communication between downstream and upstream and vice-versa also needs to get better. During the development of a distribution, many of the upstream versions are also under development, and they already have a list of known bugs. If I am a tester of Firefox through Ubuntu, I would love to have a list of known bugs as soon as the new package gets to the archive. This could be done by having an acknowledged syntax for release notes, that could then get easily parsed and bugs automatically filed and connected to the upstream bugs. Again, all of this information should be easily available to the tester, without leaving the desktop.

Testing, if done this way, would allow the tester to concentrate on the things that really matter and that make testing a skilled activity; concentrate on the hidden bugs that have not been found yet, on the special configurations and environments, on generating new ways to break the software. On having fun while testing.

Wrapping up

From what I have seen in the latest three years, testing has improved a lot in Ubuntu and the rest of Free Software projects that I am somehow involved with, but this is not enough. If we really want to increase the quality Free Software we need to start investing in testing and innovating the ways we do it, the same way we invest in development. We cannot test 21st century software with 20th century testing techniques. We need to react. Free Software is good because it is open source is not enough anymore. Free Software will be good because it is open source and has the best quality that we can offer.

14. Kick, Push

Andre Klapper

In real life, Andre Klapper is a bugmaster. During lunch break or while sleeping he works on random things in GNOME (bugsquad, release team, translation, documentation, etc) or Maemo, or studies, or eats ice cream.

At the very beginning I only had one question: How can I print a part of the email which I received in Gnome's email client Evolution? I asked on the corresponding mailing list.

I had switched to Linux exactly one year ago, out of frustration that I could not make my modem work after reinstalling a proprietary operating system that was popular around that time.

The answer to my question was "not possible". Cool kids would have checked out the code, compiled it, hacked it to make it act as wanted, and submitted a patch attached to a bug report by then. Well, as you can guess I was not a cool kid. My programming skills are rather limited, so I stuck to a cumbersome printing workaround for the time being. The answer I received on the mailing list also mentioned that the feature was in planning, and that a bug report had been filed on my behalf (without mentioning where, but I did not care about that – I was happy that there were plans to fix my issue soon).

It may just have been my laziness to have stayed subscribed to the mailing list. Some folks mentioned the bug tracker from time to time, often as a direct response to feature requests, so I took a look at it eventually. But bug trackers, especially Bugzilla, are strange tools with lots of complex options. An area you normally prefer to avoid unless you are a masochist. They contain many tickets describing bugs or feature requests by users and developers. It looked as if those reports were partially also used for planning priorities. (Calling this "Project Management" would be an euphemism - less than one fourth of the issues that were planned to get fixed or implemented for a specific release actually got fixed in the end.)

What I found beside an interesting look at the issues of the software and the popularity of certain requests were inconsistencies and some noise, like lots of duplicates or bug reports missing enough information to get processed properly. I felt like cleaning up a bit by "triaging" the available bug reports. I do not know what this tells you about my mindset though – add wrong buzzwords for random characteristics here, like organized, persistent or knowledgeable. Also nice irony considering that my father always used to complain about my messy room.

So back in those dial-up modem times I usually collected my questions and went online to enter IRC once a day in order to shoot my questions at Evolution's bugmaster who was always welcoming, patient and willing to share his experience. If there was a triaging guide available at that time covering basic bug management knowledge and explaining good practices and common pitfalls, I had not heard about it.

The amount of open reports decreased by 20% within a few months though that was of course not just because of one person starting to triage some tickets. Obviously there was some work waiting to get picked up by somebody – like decreasing the amount of open tickets for the developers so that they could better focus, discussing and setting some priorities with them, and responding to some users' comments that had remained unanswered at that time. Open Source is always welcoming to contributions once you have found your hook to participate.

Way later I realized that there is some documentation around to dive into. Luis Villa - who might have been the first bugmaster ever – wrote an essay called "Why Everyone Needs A Bugmaster"[1],

[1] `http://tieguy.org/talks-files/LCA-2005-paper-html/index.html`

and most Bugsquad teams in Open Source projects were publishing triaging guides in the meantime that helped newbies get involved in the community. Many Open Source developers started their great Open Source careers by triaging bugs and gained initial experience in software project management.

Nowadays there are also tools which can save you a lot of time when it comes to the repetitive grunt work part of triaging. On the server side GNOME's "stock answers" extension provides common and frequently used comments to add to tickets via one click, and on the client side you can run your own Greasemonkey scripts or Matěj Cepl's Jetpack extension called "bugzilla-triage-scripts"[2].

If you are an average or poor musician but still love music more than anything else, you can stick around in the business as a journalist. Software development also has such niches apart from the default idea of writing code that can make you happy. You have to spend some time to find them but it is worth the efforts, experience and contacts, and with some luck and skills it might even earn you a living in your personal field of interest and keep you from ending up as a code monkey.

[2] `https://fedorahosted.org/bugzilla-triage-scripts`

15. Test-Driven Enlightenment

Jonathan "Duke" Leto

Jonathan "Duke" Leto is a software developer, published mathematician, Git ninja and avid bicyclist living in Portland, Oregon. He is a core developer of Parrot Virtual Machine and founder of Leto Labs LLC.

When I first got involved in Free and Open Source Software, I had no clue what tests were or why they were important. I had worked on some personal programming projects before, but the first time I actually worked on a project with others, i.e., got a commit bit, was Yacas, Yet Another Computer Algebra System, a computer algebra system similar to Mathematica.

At this stage in my journey, tests were an afterthought. My general meta-algorithm was to hack on code → see if it works → write a simple test to show it works (optional). If a test was challenging to write, it most likely never got written.

This is the first step in the path to Test-Driven Enlightenment. You know tests are probably a good idea, but you have not seen the benefit of them clearly, so you only write tests occasionally.

If I could open up a wormhole and tell my younger self one piece of wisdom about testing, it would be:

> "Some tests, in the long-run, are more important than the code they test."

A few people right about now may be thinking that I put on my tinfoil testing hat when I sit down to code. How can tests be *more* important than the code they test? Tests are the proof that your code *actually* works, and they guide you to writing correct code as well as providing the flexibility to change code and know that features still work. The larger your codebase becomes, the more valuable your tests are, because they allow you to change one part of your code and still be sure that the rest of it works.

Another vital reason to write tests is because it indicates that something is explicitly desirable, rather than an unintended side-effect or oversight. If you have a specification, you can use tests to verify that you meet it, which is very valuable, and in some industries, necessary. A test is just like telling a story, where the story is how you think code should work.

Code either changes and evolves or bitrots[1].

Very often, you will write tests once, but then totally refactor your implementation or even rewrite it from scratch. Tests often outlive the code they originally tested, i.e., one set of tests can be used no matter how many times your code is refactored. Tests are actually the litmus test that allows you to throw away an old implementation and say "this newer implementation has a much better design and passes our test suite." I have seen this happen many times in the Perl and Parrot communities, where you can often find me.

Tests allow you to change things quickly and know if something is broken. They are like jet packs for developers.

Carpenters have a bit of sage wisdom that goes like this:

> "Measure twice, cut once."

Coding is like cutting and tests are like measuring.

Test-Driven Enlightenment saves an enormous amount of time, because instead of flailing around, fiddling with code, not having a direction, tests hone your focus.

Tests also are very good positive feedback. Every time you make a new test pass, you know that your code is better and it has one more feature or one less bug.

[1] The term "bitrot" is coder slang for the almost universal fact that if a piece of code does not change but everything it relies on does, it "rots" and usually has very little chance of working unless modifications are made to accommodate newer software and hardware.

It is easy to think "I want to add 50 features" and spend all day fiddling with code, constantly switching between working on different things. Most of the time, very little will be accomplished. Test-Driven Enlightenment guides one to focus on making one test pass at a time.

If you have a single failing test, you are on a mission to make it pass. It focuses your brain on something very specific, which very often has better results than switching between tasks constantly.

Most information about being test-driven is very specific to a language or situation, but that does not need to be the case. Here is the how to approach adding a new feature or fixing a bug in any language:

1. Write a test that fails, which you think will pass when the feature is implemented or bug is fixed. Advanced: As you write the test, run it occasionally, even if it is not done yet, and guess the actual error message that the test will give. The more tests you write and run, the easier this will become.

2. Hack on the code.

3. Run the test. If it passes, go to #4, otherwise go to #2.

4. You are done! Do a happy dance :)

This method works for any kind of test and any language. If you remember only one thing about testing from this essay, remember the steps above.

Here are some more general test-driven guidelines that will serve you well and apply in almost any situation:

1. Understand the difference between what is being tested and what is being used as a tool to test something else.

2. Fragile tests. You could write a test that makes sure an error message is exactly correct. But what happens when the error message changes? What happens when someone internationalizes your code to Catalan? What happens when someone runs

your code on an operating system you have never heard of? The more resilient your test is, the more valuable it will be.

Think about these things when you write tests. You want them to be resilient, i.e., tests, for the most part, should only have to change when functionality changes. If you have to change your tests often, but functionality is not changing, you are doing something wrong.

Kinds of tests

Many people start to get confused when people speak of integration tests, unit tests, acceptance tests and many other flavors of tests. One should not worry too much about these terms. The more tests you write, the more nuances you will see and the differences between tests will become more apparent. Everyone does not have the same definition for what these tests are, but the terms are still useful to describe kinds of tests.

Unit tests vs. integration tests

Unit tests and integration tests form a spectrum. Unit tests test small bits of code, and integration tests verify how more than one unit fits together. The test writer gets to decide what comprises a unit, but most often it is at the level of a function or method, although some languages call those things by different names.

To make this a little more concrete, we will give a basic analogy using functions. Imagine that $f(x)$ and $g(x)$ are two functions which represent two units of code. For concreteness, let's assume they represent two specific functions in your favorite Free/Open Source project's codebase.

An integration test asserts something like function composition, i.e., $f(g(a)) = b$. An integration test is testing how multiple things integrate or work together, instead of how a single part works individually. If algebra isn't your thing, another way to look at it is unit tests only test one part of the machine at a time, but integration tests very many parts work in unison. A great example of an integration test is test-driving a car. You are not checking the air pressure, or measuring voltage of the spark plugs. You are making sure the vehicle works as a whole.

Most of the time it is good to have both. I often start with unit tests and add integration tests as needed, since you will weed out the most basic bugs first, then find more subtle bugs that are related to how pieces do not quite fit together, as opposed to the individual pieces not working. Many people write integration tests first and then delve into unit tests. Which you write first is not nearly as important as writing both kinds.

Enlightenment

Test-Driven Enlightment is a path, not a place. Enjoy the journey and make sure to stop and smell the flowers if and when you get lost.

Part VII.

Documentation and Support

16. Life-Changer Documentation for Novices

Atul Jha

Atul Jha has been using Free Software since 2002. He is working as an Application Specialist at CSS Corp, Chennai, India. He loves visiting colleges, meeting students and spreading the word about Free Software.

In 2002, the cyber cafe was the place to surf Internet as dial up connections were very costly. During that time, Yahoo chat was very popular and I used to visit the #hackers channel there. There were some crazy people there who said they would hack my password. I was very eager to know more about hacking and become one of them. The next day I went to the cyber cafe again and typed "how to become a hacker" on Yahoo search. The very first URL was of Eric S. Raymond. I was jumping with joy that I had the magic key.

I started reading the book and to my surprise the definition of hacker was "someone who likes solving problems and overcoming limits". It also said "hackers build things, crackers break them." Alas I wanted to be a cracker but this book brought me to the other world of hacking. I kept reading the book and encountered various new terms like GNU/Linux, mailing list, Linux user group, IRC, Python and many more.

After searching further, I was able to find a Linux user group in Delhi and got a chance to meet real hackers. I felt like I was in an alien world as they were talking about Perl, RMS, the kernel, device drivers, compilation and many other things which were going over my head.

I was in a different world. I preferred coming back home and finding some Linux distribution from somewhere. I was too scared to ask for one from them. I was nowhere near their level, a total dumb newbie. I managed to get some distribution by paying 1000 Rs to a guy who used to have a business selling distribution media. I tried many of them and was not able to get my sound working. This time I decided to visit an IRC channel from the cyber cafe. I found #linux-india and jumped over asking "my sound nt wrking", then came instructions like "no SMS speak" and "RTFM". It scared me more and took some time to figure out that RTFM meant "read the f*** manual".

I was terrified and preferred staying away from IRC for a few weeks.

One fine day I got an email about a monthly Linux user group meetup. I needed answers for my many questions. I met Karunakar there and he asked me to bring my computer to his office as he had the whole Debian repository available there. Debian was new for me but I was satisfied with the fact that finally I will be able to play music on Linux. The next day I was in his office after carrying my computer on the over-crowded bus – it was fun. In a few hours, Debian was up and running on my system. He also gave me a few books for beginners and a command reference.

The next day again in the cyber cafe, I read another of Eric S. Raymond's essay called *How To Ask Questions The Smart Way.* I was still visiting the #hackers channel on Yahoo chat where I made a very good friend, Krish, who suggested me to buy a book called *Linux Command Reference.* After spending some time with those books and looking things up at tldp.org I was a newbie Linux user. I never looked back. I also attended a Linux conference where I met a few hackers from Yahoo and I was really inspired after attending their talk. Later after a few years I had a chance to meet Richard Stallman who is more like a god for many people in Free Software community.

I would admit that the documentation of Eric S. Raymond changed my life and that of many others for sure. After all these years in the

Free Software community, I have realized documentation is the key for participation of newbies in this awesome Open Source community. My 1$ advice to all developers would be to please document even the smallest work you do as the world is full of newbies who would love to read it. My blog has even simple postings like enabling the spell checker in OpenOffice to installing Django in a virtual environment.

17. Good Manners Matter

Rich Bowen

Rich Bowen has been working on Free/Open Source Software for about 15 years. Most of this time has been spent on the Apache HTTP Server, but he has also worked on Perl, PHP, and a variety of web applications. He is the author of Apache Cookbook, The Definitive Guide to Apache mod_rewrite, and a variety of other books, and makes frequent appearances at various technology conferences.

I started working on the Apache HTTP Server documentation project in September of 2000. At least, that is when I made my first commit to the docs. Prior to that, I had submitted a few patches via email, and someone else had committed them.

Since that time, I have made a little over a thousand changes to the Apache HTTP Server docs, along with just a handful of changes to the server code itself.

People get involved in Free/Open Source Software for a lot of different reasons. Some are trying to make a name for themselves. Most are trying to "scratch an itch", as the saying goes – trying to get the software to do something that it does not currently do, or create a new piece of software to fill a need that they have.

I got involved in software documentation because I had been roped into helping write a book, and the existing documentation was pretty awful. So, in order to make the book coherent, I had to talk with various people on the project to help make sense of the documentation. In the process of writing the book, I made the documentation better, purely to make my work easier.

Around that same time, Larry Wall, the creator of the Perl programming language, was promoting the idea that the three primary virtues of a programmer were laziness, impatience and hubris. Larry was making very valid points, and Larry has a sense of humor. A significant portion of the programmer community, however, take his words as license to be jerks.

What I have learned over my years in Open Source documentation is that the three primary virtues of a documentation specialist, and, more generally, of customer support, are laziness, patience, and humility. And that the over-arching virtue that ties these all together is respect.

Laziness

We write documentation so that we do not have to answer the same questions every day for the rest of our lives. If the documentation is inadequate, people will have difficulty using the software. While this may be a recipe for a lucrative consulting business, it is also a recipe for a short-lived software project, as people will give up in frustration and move on to something that they do not have to spend hours figuring out.

Thus, laziness is the first virtue of a documentation writer.

When a customer asks a question, we should answer that question thoroughly. Exhaustively, even. We should then record that answer for posterity. We should illuminate it with examples, and, if possible, diagrams and illustrations. We should make sure that the prose is clear, grammatically correct, and eloquent. We should then add this to the documentation in a place that is easy to find, and copiously cross referenced from everywhere that someone might look for it.

The next time someone asks this same question, we can answer them with a pointer to the answer. And questions that they may have after reading what has already been written should be the source of enhancements and annotations to what has already been written.

This is the true laziness. Laziness does not mean merely shirking work. It means doing the work so well that it never has to be done again.

Patience

There is a tendency in the technical documentation world to be impatient and belligerent. The sources of this impatience are numerous. Some people feel that, since they had to work hard to figure this stuff out, you should to. Many of us in the technical world are self-taught, and we have very little patience for people who come after us and want a quick road to success.

I like to refer to this as the "get off my lawn" attitude. It is not very helpful.

If you cannot be patient with the customer, then you should not be involved in customer support. If you find yourself getting angry when someone does not get it, you should perhaps let someone else take the question.

Of course, that is very easy to say, and a lot harder to do. If you find yourself in the position of being an expert on a particular subject, people are inevitably going to come to you with their questions. You are obliged to be patient, but how do you go about achieving this? That comes with humility.

Humility

I had been doing technical support, particularly on mailing lists, for about two years, when I first started attending technical conferences. Those first few years were a lot of fun. Idiots would come onto a mailing list, and ask a stupid question that a thousand other losers had asked before them. If they had taken even two minutes to just look, they would have found all the places the question had been answered before. But they were too lazy and dumb to do that.

Then I attended a conference, and discovered a few things.

First, I discovered that the people asking these questions were people. They were not merely a block of monospaced black text on a white background. They were individuals. They had kids. They had hobbies. They knew so much more than I did about a whole range of things. I met brilliant people for whom the technology was a tool to accomplish something non-technical. They wanted to share their recipes with other chefs. They wanted to help children in west Africa learn how to read. They were passionate about wine, and wanted to learn more. They were, in short, smarter than I am, and my arrogance was the only thing between them and further success.

When I returned from that first conference, I saw the users mailing list in an entirely different light. These were no longer idiots asking stupid questions. These were people who needed just a little bit of my help so that they could get a task done, but, for the most part, their passions were not technology. Technology was just a tool. So if they did not spend hours reading last year's mailing list archives, and chose instead to ask the question afresh, that was understandable.

And, surely, if on any given day it is irritating to have to help them, the polite thing to do is to step back and let someone else handle the question, rather than telling them what an imbecile they are. And, too, to remember all of the times I have had to ask the stupid questions.

Politeness and Respect

In the end, this all comes down to politeness and respect. Although I have talked mainly here about technical support, the documentation is simply a static form of technical support. It answers the questions that you expect people to have, and it provides these answers in a semi-permanent form for reference.

When writing this documentation, you should attempt to strike the balance between assuming that your reader is an idiot, and assuming that they should already know everything. At the one end, you are telling them to make sure their computer is plugged in. At the other end you are using words like "simply" and "just" to make it sound like every task is trivial, leaving the reader feeling that they are probably not quite up to the task.

This involves having a great deal of respect and empathy for your reader, and endeavoring to remember what it was like to be in the beginner and intermediate stages of learning a new software package. Examples of bad documentation are so prevalent, however, that this should not be a terribly difficult memory to rekindle. Chances are that you have felt that way within the last week.

I wish ...

I wish that when I started working on Open Source documentation I had been less arrogant. I look back at some of the things that I have said on publicly-archived mailing lists, forever enshrined on the Internet, and am ashamed that I could be that rude.

The greatest human virtue is politeness. All other virtues flow from it. If you cannot be polite, then all of the things that you accomplish amount to little.

18. Documentation and My Former Self

Anne Gentle

Anne Gentle is the fanatical technical writer and community documentation coordinator at Rackspace for OpenStack, an open source cloud computing project. Prior to joining OpenStack, Anne worked as a community publishing consultant, providing strategic direction for professional writers who want to produce online content with wikis with user-generated pages and comments. Her enthusiasm for community methods for documentation prompted her to write a book about using social publishing techniques for technical documentation titled Conversation and Community: The Social Web for Documentation. She also volunteers as a documentation maintainer for FLOSS Manuals, which provides open source documentation for open source projects.

An intriguing premise – spill my guts about what I wish I knew about open source and documentation. Rather than tell you what I wish you knew about open source and documentation, I must tell you what I wish my former self knew. The request evokes a sense of regret or remorse or even horrified notions of "What was I thinking?"

In my case, my former self was just five years younger than now, a thirty-something established professional. In contrast, others may recall their first experiences with open source as a teenager. Jono Bacon in his book, *Art of Community*, recounts standing in front of an apartment door with his heart pounding, about to meet someone he had only talked to online through an open source community. I have experienced that first in-person meeting with people I have only met online, but my first serious foray into the world of open source documentation came when I responded to an emailed request for help. The email was from a former coworker, asking for documentation help on the XO laptop, the charter project for One Laptop Per Child. I pondered the perceived opportunity, talking to my friends and spouse, wondering if it would be a good chance to experiment with new doc techniques and try something I had never done before, wiki-based documentation. Since that first experimentation, I have joined OpenStack, an open source project for cloud computing software, working full time on community documentation and support efforts.

I immediately think of the many contradictions I have found along the way. I have uncovered surprising points and counterpoints for each observation. For example, documentation absolutely matters for support, education, adoption, yet, an open source community will march on despite a lack of documentation or completely flawed docs. Another seeming juxtaposition of values is that documentation should be a good onboarding task, a starting point for new volunteers, yet new community members know so little that they can not possibly write or even edit effectively, nor are newbies familiar with the various audiences served by doc. Word on the street lately is that "developers should write developer docs" because they know the audience well and can serve others like themselves best. In my experience, new, fresh eyes are welcome to the project and some people are able to write down and share with others those fresh, empathetic eyes. You do not want to create a "newbies-only" culture around docs, though, because it is important that the key technical community members support doc efforts with their contributions and encourage others to do so.

A bit of a dirty little secret for documentation related to open source projects is that the lines drawn between official docs and unofficial doc projects are blurred at best. I wish I had known that documentation efforts get forked all the time, and new web sites can sprout up where there were none. Sprawling docs do not offer the most efficient way for people to learn about the project or software, but a meandering walk through a large set of web documentation might be more telling to those who want to read between the lines and interpret what is going on in the community through the documentation. Lots of forking and multiple audiences served may mean that the product is complex and serves many. It also can mean that no strong core documentation ethos exists in the community, so unorchestrated efforts are the norm.

I wish when I started that I had some ability to gather the "social weather" of an online community. When you walk into a restaurant with white tablecloths and couples dining and a low-level volume of conversations, the visual and auditory information you receive sets the ambiance and gives you certain clues about what to expect from your dining experience. You can translate this concept of social weather to online communities as well. An open source community gives certain clues in their mailing lists, for example. A list landing page prefixed with a lot of rules and policy around posting will be heavy in governance. A mailing list that has multiple posts emphasizing that "there are no dumb questions" is more approachable for new doc writers. I also wish I knew of a way to not only do a content audit – a listing of the content available for the open source project – but also to do a community audit – a listing of the influential members in the open source community, be they contributors or otherwise.

Lastly, an observation about open source and doc that I have enjoyed validating is the concept that documentation can occur in "sprints" – in short bursts of energy with a focused audience and outline and resulting in a known set of documentation. I was so happy to hear at a talk at SXSW Interactive that sprints are perfectly acceptable for online collaboration and you could expect lags in energy level, and that is okay. Software documentation is often fast and furious in the winding-down-days of a release cycle, and that is acceptable in open source, community-based documentation. You can be strategic and coordinated and still offer a high-energy event around documentation. These are exciting times in open source, and my former self felt it! It is a good thing you can keep learning and growing your former self into your current self with the collection of advice to tote along with you.

19. Stop Worrying and Love the Crowd

Shaun McCance

Shaun McCance has been involved in GNOME documentation since 2003 as a writer, community leader, and tool developer. He has spent most of that time wondering how to get more people to write better documentation, with some success along the way. He offers his experience in community documentation through his consulting company, Syllogist.

Something big happened as I was preparing to write this: GNOME 3 was released. This was the first major GNOME release in nine years. Everything was different, and all of the existing documentation had to be rewritten. At the same time, we were changing the way we write documentation. We had thrown away our old manuals and started fresh with dynamic, topic-oriented help using Mallard.

A few weeks before the release, a group of us got together to work on the documentation. We worked all day, planning, writing, and revising. We wrote hundreds of pages against a moving target of late-cycle software changes. We had people contributing remotely, submitting new pages and correcting existing content. It was the most productive I had ever seen our documentation team.

What did we finally get right? A lot of factors came together, and I could write an entire book about all the nuances of Open Source documentation. But the most important thing I did was get out of the way and let others do the work. I learned to delegate, and to delegate the right way.

Rewind eight years. I began to get involved with GNOME documentation in 2003. I did not have any real experience as a technical writer at the time. My day job had me working on publications tools, and I started working on the tools and help viewer used for GNOME documentation. It was not long before I was pulled into writing.

In those days, much of our documentation was handled by professional tech writers inside Sun. They would take on a manual, write it, review it, and commit it to our CVS repository. We could all look at it after the fact, learn from it, and make corrections to it. But there was no concerted effort to involve people in the writing process.

It is not that the Sun writers were trying to be protective or hide things behind closed doors. These were professional tech writers. They knew how to do their job. They were good at it. Other people could take on other manuals, but they would write their assignments the way they knew how. Running each page by a group of untrained contributors, however enthusiastic, is inviting the very worst kind of bikeshedding[1] imaginable. It is just not productive.

Inevitably, the winds shifted inside Sun and their tech writers were assigned to other projects. That left us without our most prolific and knowledgeable writers. Worse than that, we were left with no community, nobody to pick up the pieces.

There are ideas and processes that are standard in the corporate world. I have worked in the corporate world. I do not think anybody questions these ideas. People do their job. They take assignments and finish them. They ask others for reviews, but they do not farm out their work to newcomers and less experienced writers. The best writers will probably write the most.

These are all really obvious ideas, and they fail miserably in a community-based project. You will never develop a community of contributors if you do everything yourself. In a software project, you might get contributors who are skilled and persistent enough to contribute. In documentation, that almost never happens.

Most people who try to contribute to documentation do not do it because they want to be tech writers, or even because they love to write. They do it because they want to contribute, and documenta-

[1] `https://secure.wikimedia.org/wiktionary/en/wiki/bikeshedding`

tion is the only way they think they know how. They do not know how to code. They are not good at graphic design. They are not fluent enough in another language to translate. But they know how to write.

This is where professional writers roll their eyes. The fact that you are literate does not mean you can write effective user documentation. It is not just about putting words on paper. You need to understand your users, what they know, what they want, where they are looking. You need to know how to present information in a way they will understand, and where to put it so they will actually find it.

Tech writers will tell you that tech writing is not something just anybody can do. They are right. And that is exactly why the most important thing professional writers can do for the community is not write.

The key to building a successful documentation community is to let others make the decisions, do the work, and own the results. It is not enough to just give them busy work. The only way they will care enough to stick around is if they are personally invested. A sense of ownership is a powerful motivator.

But if you only get inexperienced writers, and you hand all the work over to them, how can you ensure you create quality documentation? Uncontrolled crowd-sourcing does not create good results. The role of an experienced writer in a community is as a teacher and mentor. You have to teach them to write.

Start by involving people early in the planning. Always plan from the bottom up. Top-down planning is not conducive to collaboration. It is hard to involve people in crafting a high-level overview when not everybody has the same sense of what goes into that overview. But people can think of the pieces. They can think about individual topics to write, tasks people perform, problems people have, questions people ask. They can look at forums and mailing lists to see what users ask.

Write a few pages yourself. It gives people something to imitate. Then dish out everything else. Let other people own topics, or entire groups of topics. Make it clear what information they need to provide, but let them write. People will learn by doing.

Be constantly available to help them out and answer questions. At least half the time I spend on documentation is spent answering questions so that other people can get work done. When people submit drafts, review the drafts and discuss critiques and corrections with them. Do not just make the corrections yourself.

This still leaves you handling the big picture. People are filling in parts of the puzzle, but you are still putting it together. As people get more experienced, they will naturally take bigger and bigger pieces. Encourage people to get more involved. Give them more to do. Get them to help you help more writers. The community will run itself.

Eight years later, GNOME has managed to create a documentation team that runs itself, deals with problems, makes decisions, produces great documentation, and constantly brings in new contributors. Anybody can join in and make a difference, and that is the key to a successful Open Source community.

Part VIII.

Translation

20. My Project Taught Me how to Grow Up

Runa Bhattacharjee

For the past 10 years, Runa Bhattacharjee has been translating and working on localizing numerous Open Source projects - ranging from Desktop interfaces to Operating System tools and lots of things in between. She strongly believes that upstream repositories are the best places to submit any form of changes. She also holds a professional portfolio specializing in Localization, at Red Hat. Runa translates and maintains translations for Bengali (Indian version), but is always happy to help anyone wanting to get started with localization.

Introduction

Burning the midnight oil has been a favorite form of rebellion by young people all over the world. Whether to read a book with a torchlight under the covers or to watch late night TV reruns or (amongst other things) to hang around on an IRC channel and tinkering around with an itchy problem with a favorite open source project.

How it all began

That is how it all began for me. Let me first write a bit about myself. When I got introduced to the local Linux Users Group in my city, I was in between jobs and studying for a masters degree. Very soon I was a contributor to a few localization projects and started translating (mostly) desktop interfaces. We used a few customized editors with integrated writing methods and fonts. The rendering engines had not matured well enough to display the script with zero errors on the interfaces, nonetheless we kept on translating. My focus was on the workflow that I had created for myself. I used to get the translatable content from the folks who knew how things work, translate it as best as I could, add in the comments to help the reviewers understand how I comprehended the text, filled in the necessary information for copyright and credits and sent them back to the coordinators.

How it was done

It was mostly a simple way of doing things. But most importantly it was *my* independent way of doing things. I took my own time to schedule when I would work on the translations. These would then be reviewed and returned to me for changes. Again, I would schedule them for completion as per how I could squeeze out some time from all the studying and other work that I was doing. When I did get down to work, I would sit through 9-10 straight hours mostly into the wee hours of the morning, feeling a high of accomplishment until the next assignments came through.

What mattered

What I did not know was that I played a significant part in the larger scheme of things. Namely, release schedules. So, when I completed my 2 cents of the task and sent them over, I did not factor in a situation where they could be rendered useless because they were too late for the current release and too early for the next release (which would invariably contain a lot of changes that would require a rework). Besides these, I was oblivious to the fact how it all mattered to the entire release process – integration, packaging, interface testing, bug filing, resolution.

How it made me grow up

All these changed drastically when I moved into a more professional role. So suddenly I was doing the same thing but in a more structured order. I learned that the cavalier road-rolling that I had been used to, was not scalable when one had to juggle through 2-3 release schedules. It had to be meticulously planned to map with the project roadmaps. While working on translating a desktop interface, one had to check what the translation schedule was for the main project. The projected date to start working would be right after when all the original interface messages had been frozen. Translators could then work unhindered until the translation deadline, after which they would be marked as stable in the main repositories and eventually packages would be build. Along with these schedules, a couple of operating system distributions would align their schedules as well. So the translators had the additional responsibility of making sure that the pre-release versions of the operating system that would be carrying the desktop, went through with some bits of testing to ensure that the translations made sense on the interface and did not contain errors.

What I should have known

The transition was not easy. Suddenly there was a flood of information that I had to deal with and additional chores that I had to perform. From being a hobby and more importantly a stress-buster, suddenly it was serious business. Thinking in retrospect, I can say that it probably helped me understand the entire process because I had to learn it from the ground up. And armed with that knowledge I can analyze situations with a better understanding of all the effective facets. At the time when I started working on the Open Source project(s) of my interest, there were much fewer professionals who worked full time in this domain. Most of the volunteer contributors held day jobs elsewhere and saw these projects as a way to nurture the creative juices that had dried up in their routine tasks. So a number of newcomers were never mentored about how to plan out their projects professionally. They grew to be wonderfully skilled in what they were doing and eventually figured out how they would like to balance their work with the rest of the things they were doing.

Conclusion

These days I mentor newcomers and one of the first things that I let them know is how and in which part of the project they matter. Crafting an individual style of work is essential as it allows a person a comfortable space to work in, but an understanding of the organized structure that is affected by their work imbibes the discipline that is required to hold in check chances of arbitrary caprice.

Part IX.

Usability

21. Learn from Your Users

Guillaume Paumier

Guillaume Paumier is a photographer and physicist living in Toulouse, France. A long-time Wikipedian, he currently works for the Wikimedia Foundation, the non-profit that runs Wikipedia. As a product manager for Multimedia Usability, he notably conducted user research to design a new media upload system for Wikimedia Commons, the free media library associated with Wikipedia.

You know Wikipedia, the freely reusable encyclopedia that anyone can edit? It was created in 2001 and recently celebrated its tenth anniversary. Despite being one of the ten most visited websites in the world, its user interface still looks very "1.0' compared to what interactive web technologies allow. Some might say it is for the best: Wikipedia is "serious stuff", and the user should not be distracted by "fireworks" in the interface. Yet, Wikipedia has had issues recruiting new contributors in the last few years, in part because of its interface that some may call archaic. This might explain why surveys of Wikipedia participants have repeatedly shown a bias towards young, technology-savvy men, many with a background in computers and engineering. Besides the fact that free knowledge and free licenses sprouted from the fertile land of Free and Open Source Software, the complicated interface has discouraged many motivated potential participants.

In 2011, while major online publishing and collaboration platforms (like WordPress, Etherpad and Google Documents) offer a visual editor to some extent, Wikipedia still uses by default an old-fashioned wikitext editor that uses quotes ('''') and brackets ([[]]) for formatting. Efforts are underway to transition to a default visual editor in 2012, but it is not an easy challenge to solve.

But let us put the editor aside for a moment. The interface of Wikipedia remains fairly complicated, and many useful features are difficult to discover. Did you know Wikipedia has an integrated version control system, and you can see all the previous versions of a page? Did you know you can see the list of all the edits made by a participant? Did you know you can link to a specific version of a page? Did you know you can export a page to PDF, or create custom hardcover books from Wikipedia content, to be sent to your home?

The Implementation Model

Most Wikipedia readers arrive through search engines. Statistics show they spend little time on Wikipedia once they find the information they were looking for. Few stick around and explore what tools the interface offers. For example, Wikipedia is routinely criticized about its quality and reliability. Many of these unexplored, almost hidden tools could prove useful to readers to help them assess the reliability of information.

Wikipedia and its sister projects (like Wikisource and Wikimedia Commons) are powered by a wiki engine called MediaWiki (and supported by the Wikimedia Foundation; all these confusing names alone are a usability sin). For a long time, the development of MediaWiki was primarily led by software developers. The MediaWiki community has a strong developer base; actually, this community is almost entirely composed of developers. Only recently did designers join the community and they were hired by the Wikimedia Foundation in this capacity. There are hardly any volunteer designers in the community. This has caused the application to be built and "designed" exclusively by developers. As a consequence, the interface has naturally taken a shape that closely follows the "implementation model", i.e., the way the software is implemented in the code and data structures. Only rarely does this implementation model match the "user model", i.e., the way the user imagines things to work.

It would be unfair to say that developers do not care about users. The purpose of creating software (apart from the sheer pleasure of learning stuff, writing code and solving problems) is to release it so it can be used. This is particularly true in the world of Free and Open Source Software, where most developers selflessly volunteer their time and expertise. One might argue that many developers are, in fact, users of their own products, especially in the world of Free and Open Source software. After all, they created it or joined its team, for a reason, and this reason was rarely money. As a consequence, developers of this kind of software would be in an ideal position to know what the user wants.

But let's face it: if you are reading this, you are not your regular user.

The Developer Point Of View

If you are a developer, it is particularly difficult for you to sit in the user's chair. For one thing, your familiarity with the code and the software's implementation makes you see its features and interface from a very specific perspective. You know each and every feature of the application you created. You know where to find everything. If something with the interface feels a little odd, you may unconsciously discard it because you know it is a side-effect of how you implemented such or such a feature.

Let us say you are creating an application that stores data in tabular form (possibly in a database). When the time comes to show this data to the user, you will naturally think of the data as tabular, because it is how you implemented it. It will make sense to you to display it in a way that is consistent with how it is stored. Similarly, any kind of array or other sequential structure is bound to be remembered as such, and displayed in a sequential format in the interface as well, perhaps as a list. However, another format may make more sense for the regular user, for example a set of sentences, a chart, or another visual representation.

Another challenge is your level of expertise. Because you want your application to be awesome, you are likely to do a lot of research to build it. In the end, you may not only become an expert in your application, but also an expert in your application's topic. Many of your users will not have (or need) that level of expertise, and they may be lost with the level of detail of some features, or be unfamiliar with some terms the layperson does not know.

So, what can you do to fix it?

Watch users. Seriously.

Watching people as they use your application is truly an eye-opening experience.

Now, one way to watch people use your application is to hire a usability firm, who will recruit testers with various profiles among a pool of thousands, prepare an interview script, rent a room in a usability lab with a screen-recording app, a video camera pointed at the user, and you in a backroom behind a one-way glass, head-desking and swearing every time the user does something you think does not make any sense. If you can afford to do that, then by all means, do so. What you will learn will really change your perspective. If you can not afford professional testing, all is not lost; you are just going to have to do it yourself. Just sit beside a user as they show you how they perform their tasks and go through their workflow. Be a silent observer: your goal is to observe, and note everything. Many things will surprise you. Once the user is done, you can go through your notes and ask questions to help you understand how they think.

To know more about do-it-yourself testing have a look at *Don't Make Me Think: A Common Sense Approach to Web Usability* by Steve Krug, *About Face 3: The Essentials of Interaction Design* by Alan Cooper, Robert Reimann and David Cronin, and the OpenUsability project[1]. It can be a bit awkward for users to be watched, yet I bet many of them will happily volunteer to help you improve your

[1] `http://openusability.org`

application. Users who cannot contribute code are usually happy to find other ways to participate in Free Software, and showing you how they use the software is a very easy way to do so. Users are generally grateful for the time you have spent developing the application, and they want to give back.

You will need to keep in mind, that not everything your users request can or should be done. Listen carefully to their stories: it is an opportunity for you to identify issues. But just because a user requests a feature does not mean they really need that feature; perhaps the best way to fix the issue underlying their feature request is to implement a completely different feature. Take what your users say with a grain of salt. But you probably knew that already.

Oh, and by the way, do not ask your family, either.

No offense intended, I am sure your mom, dad, sisters and brothers are very nice people. But if you are creating an accounting application, and your sister has never done any accounting, she is going to be quite lost. You will spend more time explaining what double-entry bookkeeping is than really testing your software. However, your mom, who bought herself a digital camera last year, could be an ideal tester if you are creating an application to manage digital photos, or to upload them to a popular online sharing platform. For your accounting application, you could ask one of your colleagues or friends who already knows a thing or two about accounting.

Ask different people, too.

For some cosmological reason, people will find endless ways to use and abuse your application, and break it in ways you would not think of in your worst nightmares. Some will implement processes and workflows with your application that make absolutely no sense to you, and you will want to slam your head on your desk. Others will use your application in ways so smart, they will make you feel stupid. Try to listen to users with different profiles, who have different goals when they use your application.

Users are an unpredictable species. But they are on your side. Learn from them.

If you remember nothing else, ...

... then remember this:

- You will be tempted to make the interface look and behave like how it works in the back-end. Your users can help you prevent that.
- Users are an unpredictable species. They will break, abuse and optimize your application in ways you can not even imagine.
- Learn from your users. Improve your application based on what you learned. Profit.

22. Software that Has the Quality Without A Name

Federico Mena Quintero

Federico Mena Quintero is one of the founders of the GNOME project, and was the maintainer of the GIMP some time before that. He worked at Red Hat Advanced Development Labs during the early days of GNOME, and later was one of the first hires at Ximian, where he worked mainly on the Evolution Calendar. He still works on GNOME in general, for Novell / Suse, and lives in Mexico.

When I was learning how to program, I noticed that I frequently hit the same problem over and over again: I would often write a program that worked reasonably well, and even had a good structure, but after some time of modifying it and enhancing it, I could no longer tweak it any further. Either its complexity would overwhelm me, or it would be so tightly written that it allowed no room for expansion, like a house where you cannot build up because it has a sloping roof, and you cannot build to the sides because it has a wall all around it.

As I got better, I learned to deal with complexity. We all learn how to do that with various tools and techniques: abstraction, encapsulation, object-orientation, functional techniques, etc. We learn how various techniques let us write broader programs.

However, the problem of having a program that was too tight or too intertwined to modify still persisted. Sometimes I had what I thought was a beautiful design, but modifying it in any way would "make it uglier" and I did not want that. Other times I had something with so many interconnected parts, that I just could not plug anything else into it or the whole thing would fall down under its own weight.

Some years ago the whole *Refactoring* craze started, but I did not pay much attention to it. I said, sure, it is a way to clean up your code, but so what? I already know how to take a chunk of code and turn it into a function; I already know how to take similar chunks of code and turn them into derived classes. I already know how to write mostly-clean code. What is the big deal?

I dismissed *Refactoring* as something suited to less experienced programmers; as some nice recipes for cleaning up your code, but nothing that you could not discover yourself.

The same thing happened to me with *Design Patterns*. I thought they were just giving pompous names like Singleton and Strategy to the everyday kinds of structures one would naturally put in a program. Maybe my ego as a programmer was too inflated to consider those works seriously. But then, something happened.

Christopher Alexander's work

Some years ago, my wife and I bought a small, one-story house and we wanted to expand it. We were thinking of having a child, so we needed more space. I needed a real home-office, not just a leftover alcove where my desk and bookcases barely fit. As avid cooks, we both needed a kitchen that was larger and more comfortable than the one the house had. My wife needed a Room Of Her Own.

We did not want to pay for an expensive architect, and neither of us knew anything about construction. How would we design our house?

At times, while browsing the web, I will sometimes remember that I have seen the name of a certain author before, or the title of a book, or something like that. I may have not really paid attention to it in the past, but somehow, the more times I see the same thing mentioned, the more likely it is that I will get interested enough in it to actually see what it is about. "Oh, several people have already mentioned this name or this book; maybe I should check it out."

That is just what happened with the name of Christopher Alexander. I had read that he was a peculiar architect (of real-world buildings, not software), somehow connected to the software world through object-oriented techniques. As I started reading about his work, I became tremendously interested in it.

In the 1970s, Christopher Alexander was a mathematician/architect teaching at the University of California, Berkeley. He and a group of like-minded architects went to various places around the world, trying to see if there were reasons for why there are human-built places in the world (cities, towns, parks, buildings, houses) where it is very pleasant to be, those that are comfortable, livable, and *nice*, and some places where this is not the case. The pleasant places were present in all of the traditional architectures of the world – European, African, Asian, American – which pointed to the idea of being able to extract common factors from all of them.

Alexander and his team distilled their findings into a list of good architectural patterns, and published three books: *The Timeless Way of Building*, where they describe the philosophy and method of good architecture; *A Pattern Language*, which I will describe next; and *The Oregon Experiment*, where they detail the design and construction of a university campus with their method.

A Pattern Language

A pattern is a recurring problem when designing and building things, with a discussion of the forces that shape the problem, and with a solution that is in turn connected, almost recursively, to other super- or sub-patterns. For example, let us consider the INTIMACY GRADIENT, an important pattern in the book (patterns are spelled in capital letters throughout the book for easy identification, so I will do the same):

INTIMACY GRADIENT

Super-patterns and preamble: ... if you know roughly where you intend to place the building wings - WINGS OF LIGHT, and how many stories they will have - NUMBER OF STORIES, and where the MAIN ENTRANCE is, it is time to work out the rough disposition of the major areas on every floor. In every building the relationship between the public areas and private areas is most important.

Statement of problem: Unless the spaces in a building are arranged in a sequence which corresponds to their degrees of privateness, the visits made by strangers, friends, guests, clients, family, will always be a little awkward.

Discussion: I will not quote all of it. But for example, consider an apartment where you can only reach the bathroom by first crossing the bedroom. Visits are always awkward because you feel like you need to tidy up your room first, if you intend your visitors to be able to use the WC! Or consider an office, where you do not want a quiet work space to be right next to the reception, because then it will not be quiet at all – you want it to be more private, towards the back.

Summary of the solution: Lay out the spaces of a building so that they create a sequence which begins with the entrance and the most public parts of the building, then leads into the slightly more private areas, and finally to the most private domains.

Sub-patterns to consult: COMMON AREAS AT THE HEART. ENTRANCE ROOM for houses; A ROOM OF ONE'S OWN for individuals. RECEPTION WELCOMES YOU for offices, HALF-PRIVATE OFFICE at the back.

The patterns get quite specific, but they never impose a style or an actual shape for the result. For example, there is a pattern called OPEN SHELVES. Deep cupboards make you put things behind other things, so you can not see them nor reach them. They also have a big footprint. Cupboards that are one-item-deep automatically stay tidy, and you always know at a glance where everything is. Things that you use frequently should not be behind doors.

So you can see the essence of design patterns: good, tested recipes that do not constrain your implementation in unnecessary ways. The patterns do not mandate a particular style, nor include superfluous decorations: the book does not tell you, "make this shape of flourishes in the handrails"; instead it tells you, "a house should have its rooms placed such that sunlight enters them according to the time of the day in which they are most used – East for the bedrooms in the morning, West for the living room in the afternoon".

I had gotten a copy of *A Pattern Language* shortly before starting the expansion of our house. The book was a revelation: **this** was the way to approach the design of our house, and now we could do it ourselves instead of paying a lot of money for an inadequate solution. We were able to make up a rough plan for our house, and then figure out smaller details as the construction went on. This is the kind of book that, as you read it, manages to confirm intuitive ideas that you half-knew you had – the kind of book where you find yourself saying, "of course, this is completely how I thought it should be" all the time.

Design Patterns, the well-known book by Gamma et al, took direct inspiration from Alexander's architectural patterns. They wanted to do the same thing: to make a list of problems that appear frequently when programming, and to present good solutions for them, that would not constrain your implementation unnecessarily.

One thing that I realized while reading *A Pattern Language* (a valuable thing from both lists of patterns, the architectural and the software one) is that they give us a vocabulary to talk about how things are constructed. It is much more convenient to say, "this object has listeners for its properties", than "this object lets you hook callback functions that are called when its properties change". What I thought were only pompous names, are in fact ways to express knowledge in a compact form.

The Quality Without A Name

Much of Alexander's discussion of patterns and their philosophy refers something which he calls the "Quality Without A Name". You know places with the Quality Without A Name. It is present in the coffee shop where you like to go to read, because the afternoon light hits it at just the right intensity, and there are comfortable seats and tables, and somehow it always is packed with people and yet you do not feel overcrowded. It is present in the corner in a park where a tree shades a bench, maybe there is some water running, and no matter if it rains or if it is sunny, it always seems to be a pleasure to be there. Think of a Hobbit House, where everything is at hand, everything is comfortable, and everything is lovingly made.

A thing or place has the Quality Without A Name if it is comfortable, has evolved over time in its own terms, is free of inner contradictions, does not try to draw attention to itself, and seems to have archetypal qualities – like if it were the way that thing was supposed to be built. Most importantly, Alexander asserted that this is an objective quality, not a subjective one, and that it can be measured and compared. Although this seems like a very vague definition, that is as far as Alexander was able to take it during this first phase of his work. The real revelation would come later.

As programmers, we have all seen beautiful programs at some point. Maybe they are the examples in *Programming Pearls*, a beautiful book which every hacker should read. Maybe you have seen a beautifully implemented algorithm that exudes rightness. Maybe you remember a very compact, very legible, very functional, very correct piece of code. That software has the Quality Without A Name.

It became clear to me that I had to learn to write software that attained the Quality Without A Name, and Alexander's frame of mind was the right starting point for this.

The ticket booth

Alexander's PhD dissertation, which was the basis for his book *Notes on the Synthesis of Form* from 1964, tried to mathematize design by defining it as a progression from a series of requirements to a final result, through an analysis of the forces that shaped the design.

Let me quote Richard Gabriel, of whom I will talk more later, when he describes the time when Alexander was trying to design a ticket booth based on his mathematical ideas:

> Alexander says [about the Quality Without A Name]:
>
> > It is a subtle kind of freedom from inner contradictions. (Alexander 1979)
>
> This statement reflects the origins of his inquiry into the quality. It started in 1964 when he was doing a study for the [San Francisco] Bay Area Rapid Transit (BART) system based on the work reported in Notes on the Synthesis of Form (Alexander 1964), which in turn was based on his Ph.D. dissertation. One of the key ideas in this book was that in a good design there must be an underlying correspondence between the structure of the problem and the structure of the solution – good design proceeds by writing down the requirements, analyzing their interactions on the basis of potential misfits, producing a hierarchical decomposition of the parts, and piecing together a structure whose
>
> > structural hierarchy is the exact counterpart of the functional hierarchy established during the analysis of the program. (Alexander 1964)
>
> Alexander was studying the system of forces surrounding a ticket booth, and he and his group had written down 390 requirements for what ought to be happening near it. Some of them pertained to such things as being there to get tickets, being able to get change, being able to move

> past people waiting in line to get tickets, and not having to wait too long for tickets. What he noticed, though, was that certain parts of the system were not subject to these requirements and that the system itself could become bogged down because these other forces - forces not subject to control by requirements – acted to come to their own balance within the system. For example, if one person stopped and another also stopped to talk with the first, congestion could build up that would defeat the mechanisms designed to keep traffic flow smooth. Of course there was a requirement that there not be congestion, but there was nothing the designers could do to prevent this by means of a designed mechanism.

As a programmer, does this sound familiar? You can make a beautiful, thorough design, that crumbles down when you actually build it because things emerge that you did not anticipate. This is not a failure of your design, but of something else! Richard Gabriel goes on:

> Alexander said this:
>
> > So it became clear that the free functioning of the system did not purely depend on meeting a set of requirements. It had to do, rather, with the system coming to terms with itself and being in balance with the forces that were generated internal to the system, not in accordance with some arbitrary set of requirements we stated. I was very puzzled by this because the general prevailing idea at the time [in 1964] was that essentially everything was based on goals. My whole analysis of requirements was certainly quite congruent with the operations research point of view that goals had to be stated and so on. What bothered me was that

> the correct analysis of the ticket booth could not be based purely on one's goals, that there were realities emerging from the center of the system itself and that whether you succeeded or not had to do with whether you created a configuration that was stable with respect to these realities.

And that is the core of the problem: how do you create a configuration that is stable with the realities that emerge from itself as you build it?

The Nature of Order

Although Christopher Alexander knew that he had produced something valuable with his investigation and catalog of patterns, he was not completely satisfied. Where had the patterns come from? Could we make new patterns from scratch, or must we be content with what traditional architecture has managed to evolve so far? Are patterns necessary at all? How can we better define, and evaluate or measure, the Quality Without A Name?

Alexander spent the next twenty years researching those questions. By studying the actual process by which good built environments had been created, he discovered that processes of a certain kind are essential to creating good towns, or buildings, or any man-made thing in fact. He arrived at the following conclusions:

- Nature creates things that all have about 15 properties in common (I will show you later). This happens solely through natural processes – standard physics and chemistry – although it is not quite clear why very different processes produce similar results.

- Traditional architectures, or towns which just evolved over time, also have those properties. You can derive all the patterns in *A Pattern Language* by following a certain process based on those properties.

- Each property can also describe a transformation to the existing space.
- The only way to achieve good design is by using those transformations, one at a time.

This was published in 2003-2004 in four volumes titled *The Nature of Order*.

The fifteen properties

The first book in *The Nature of Order* deals with fifteen properties that appear in all natural systems. I will summarize them very briefly; see the references for pictures and more extensive explanations.

- **Levels of scale:** There is a balanced range of sizes. You do not have abrupt changes in the sizes of adjacent things. Elements have fractal scale.
- **Strong centers:** You can clearly identify parts of the space or structure.
- **Thick boundaries:** Lines delimit things. In living systems, edges are the most productive environments (e.g., all the critters that live at the edge of the water).
- **Alternating repetition:** High/low, thick/thin, shape A and shape B. Things oscillate and alternate to create a good balance.
- **Positive space:** Space is beautifully shaped, convex, enclosed. It is not leftover space. Think of how a Voronoi diagram has cells that grow outward from a bunch of points, or how a piece

of corn has kernels that grow from tiny points until they touch the adjacent kernels.

- **Good shape:** The sails of a ship, the shell of a snail, the beak of a bird. They attain the optimal shape for their purpose, which is beautiful.

- **Local symmetries:** The world is not symmetrical at large. But small things tend to be symmetrical, because it is easier that way. Your house is not symmetrical, but each window is.

- **Deep interlock and ambiguity:** The crooked streets of old towns. Axons in neurons. It is hard to separate figure and ground, or foreground and background. Two strong centers are made stronger if a third center is placed between them, so that it belongs to both.

- **Contrast:** You can distinguish where one thing ends and the next one begins, because they do not fade into each other.

- **Gradients:** Things fade into each other where they need to. Concentrations in solutions, snow or earth banks, the wires that support a bridge. The way bandwidth decreases as you move away from the backbone.

- **Roughness:** The world is not frictionless and smooth. Irregularities are good because they let each piece adapt perfectly to its surroundings, rather than being an exact copy that may not fit as well.

- **Echoes:** Things repeat and echo each other. Things are unique in their exact shape, but the general shapes repeat over and over.

- **The void:** Sometimes you get a big blank area for quietness of form. A lake, a courtyard, a picture window.

- **Simplicity and inner calm:** Things are as simple as possible, but no simpler.

- **Non-separateness:** Everything depends on everything else. You cannot separate a fish from the pond and the aquatic plants. You cannot separate a column from the base of the building.

Structure-preserving transformations

The second book in *The Nature of Order* describes how each of those properties also defines a transformation. For example:

- **Thick boundaries:** You can sometimes transform something beneficially by adding a boundary to it. You plant a hedge around a garden, which then serves as beauty, as a wind-break so that strong winds do not damage the garden, and as a productive system on its own. In a graphical user interface, scrollable boxes without a frame are hard to distinguish from the window's background (think of all white web pages with text entry boxes that do not have a frame). You put a cornice at the top of a building, so that you do not get an abrupt transition between the building and the sky.

- **Local symmetries:** Small parts of built things are easier to build symmetrically; because they are turned on a lathe, because they need access from both sides, because they fold like a book. Making things asymmetrical just to be interesting takes extra work and it is harder to make them work well.

- **Positive space:** Feeling too exposed when in your desk? Add a waist-high bookshelf beside you to delimit your space, but not to completely close you off. Does your user interface feel like a lot of leftover space after you place the controls? Make the controls surround the usable space instead.

Each of these is a structure-preserving transformation. You make a change in the existing structure not by tearing it down and remaking it, but by tweaking one thing at a time according to those properties as transformations.

In software terms, it turns out that this is what much of *Refactoring* is about, when you translate the concepts to code. Refactoring is just applying structure-preserving transformations, or as Martin Fowler (the author of *Refactoring*) would put it, behavior-preserving transformations. You do not change what the program does; you just change how it is built internally, piece by piece.

By extracting a chunk of code and putting it in a function with a name, you are essentially adding a thick boundary around that code, and creating a strong center. By removing a global variable and adding class variables, you are allowing for roughness, as every instance can now have a different value in that variable, as needed. By having a producer/consumer, or notifier/listener, you have local symmetries, deep interlock and ambiguity, and good shape.

Richard Gabriel, one of the principal figures in Common Lisp, studied how to apply Alexander's theories to software (and also to poetry, and is code not similar to poetry after all?). He gives the following example:

1. Imagine that you write a PhoneCall class. This is a latent center, not as strong as it could be.

2. Gerard Meszaros, in *Pattern: Half Object + Protocol* suggested that you should split that into half calls tied by a protocol. We attain a local symmetry, we make a strong center, and get levels of scale.

3. Now make a diagram of that: You have local symmetry, levels

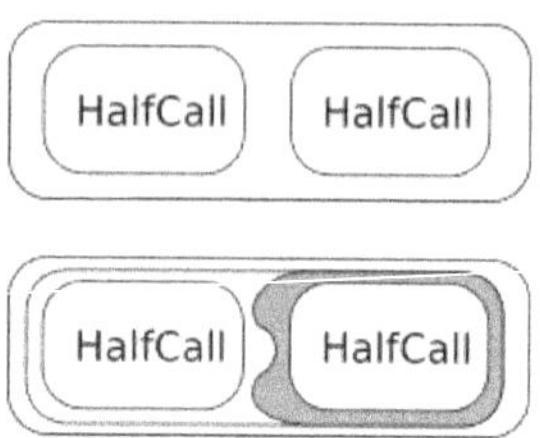

of scale, boundaries, deep interlock and ambiguity – and this is where Meszaros left things.

4. Richard Gabriel then suggests strengthening the centers that exist by applying other structure-preserving transformations. What about the latent center in the middle? You add an ex-

plicit boundary (Call) that ties the HalfCalls. This improves the local symmetries, retains deep interlock and ambiguity, and it is composable.

5. Yes, composable. Multi-way calls, conference calls, happen all

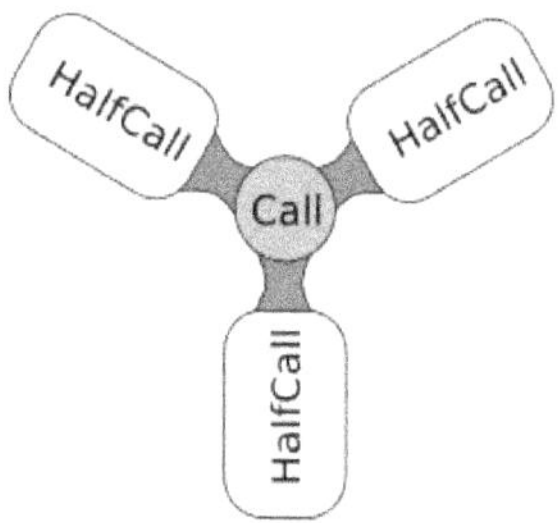

out of applying structure-preserving transformations.

Probably every programmer keeps a mental picture of the program he is creating or modifying. The hard part of modifying code that you did not write is forming that mental picture in the first place. When you work to make the code present a more beautiful picture, your code becomes better – and Alexander gives us a good way to do that.

The fundamental process

Over a long argument, Alexander explains why following this process of applying structure-preserving transformations is the **only** way to achieve a good, functional design. This is not just for buildings, but for everything we construct. It does not matter if you start with an existing program or building or city, or whether you are starting from scratch. We mimic nature's own evolutions and regenerative processes, but we do it faster.

1. Start with what you have – an empty lot, or an already-built building, or a program that looks ugly and is hard to use.

2. Identify the centers that exist in that space. Find the weakest center or the least coherent.

3. See how to apply one or more of the fifteen structure-preserving transformations to strengthen that weak center. Does it need to be delimited? Does it need to be blended with its surroundings? Does it need more detail? Does it need to be de-cluttered?

4. Find the new centers that are born when you apply the transformation to the old center. Does the new combination make things stronger? Prettier? More functional?

5. Ensure that you did the simplest possible thing.

6. Go back to the beginning for the next step.

A super-simple summary would be: find the bad parts, make them better in the simplest way possible, test the results, iterate.

Alexander is not keen on destroying things just to rebuild them in a different way. You should not demolish parts of a town to rebuild it; you should improve it gradually. In software, it is well-known that you should not rewrite things just because you do not understand them anymore. Tearing things down makes you lose all the knowledge you had embodied in the thing you are destroying, even if it looks ugly in its current state.

Similarly, Alexander is against making detailed, up-front designs. He gives a good argument of why pre-made designs can not work well in the end: because you can not predict absolutely everything that will come up during construction or implementation; because you will miss details of the environment into which your creation will live; because nature itself is not pre-ordained, and rather it grows organically and mercilessly evolves things until they manage to survive by themselves.

In this fashion, you do not design the whole user interface, or the whole structure, for a big program in a single step. You go from big to small or small to big (levels of scale); you test each part individually until it is good (strong centers); you make sure the parts are not too disconnected from each other (non-separateness). You move a few widgets where they are easier to reach, or where they are closer to the data to which they refer. You remove some frames and separators to reduce clutter. Above all, you continually evaluate what you created against real users and real use cases, so that you empirically test things against reality, not against castles in the sky.

A Name for the Quality

Over the course of *The Nature of Order*, Alexander manages to show that environments or structures that are built according to that method all end up having the Quality Without A Name. He calls this **living structure**. It can be measured and compared. It no longer has no name; we can now speak of environments with more or less living structure than others, or of programs with more or less living structure than others – and we strive to make and have more of that property.

I just called this essay, "Software that has the Quality Without A Name" because it sounds more mysterious that way.

I can not claim to know the perfect way of designing and writing software now, but at least I have a good method grounded on what produces good things elsewhere. It worked for my house, and so far I have seen it work very well for my software. I hope it works well for you, too!

References

- Christopher Alexander, *A Pattern Language.* Online version at `http://bit.ly/8n6igg`
- Christopher Alexander, *The Nature of Order.* Terrible web page at `http://www.natureoforder.com`
- Photos and drawings of the fifteen properties of life - `http://bit.ly/b82Dxu`
- Richard Gabriel, *Patterns of Software.* A beautiful, wide-ranging book on software development, Christopher Alexander's ideas, and the search for good techniques for writing software. Online version at `http://bit.ly/dqGUp4`
- Richard Gabriel, *Christopher Alexander: the search for beauty.* A very good presentation of Christopher Alexander's ideas and an exposition of patterns in the software world. `http://bit.ly/ztE6cp`
- Richard Gabriel, *The Nature of Order: the post-patterns world.* Another very good presentation, subsequent to the previous one, that explains the Fifteen Properties of Life, the Fundamental Process, and how this relates to software. `http://dreamsongs.com/Files/NatureOfOrder.pdf`

- Federico Mena Quintero, *Software that has the Quality Without A Name*. Presentation for the 2011 Desktop Summit in Berlin. `http://bit.ly/oYgJUf`

Part X.

Artwork and Design

23. Don't Be Shy

Máirín Duffy Strode

Máirín Duffy Strode has been using Free and Open Source software since she was in high school, and has been a contributor for the past 8 years. She is involved in both the Fedora and GNOME communities and has worked on interaction design, branding, and/or iconography for a number of prominent FOSS applications such as Spacewalk, Anaconda, virt-manager, SELinux and SSSD. She has also been involved in outreach efforts teaching children design skills using FOSS tools such as GIMP and Inkscape and is a fierce advocate for said tools. She is the team lead of the Fedora Design Team and a senior interaction designer with Red Hat, Inc.

I knew about and used Free and Open Source software for a long time before I became a contributor. This was not for lack of trying – there were a couple of false starts, and I succumbed to them mostly out of being too shy and afraid to push through them. From the aftermath of those false starts and also from on-boarding other designers in FOSS projects, I have five tips to offer to you as a designer trying to ramp up as a FOSS contributor:

1. Know that you are needed and wanted (badly!)

My first false start happened when I was a first-year computer science student at Rensselaer Polytechnic Institute. There was a particular project I used a lot and I wanted to get involved with it. I did not know anyone in the project (or anyone who was involved in free software) so I was trying to get involved pretty cold. The project's website indicated that they wanted help and that they had an IRC channel, so I lurked in there for a week or two. One day after a lull in conversation, I spoke up: I said I was a computer science student interested in usability and that I would love to get involved.

"Go away" was the response. Furthermore, I was told that *my* help was not needed nor wanted.

This set me back a few years in getting involved – just a few harsh words on IRC made me afraid to try again for almost 5 years. I did not discover until much later that the person who had essentially chased me out of that project's IRC channel was on the fringes of the project and had a long history of such behavior, and that I really had not done anything wrong. If I had only kept trying and talked to other people, I may have been able to get started back then.

If you would like to contribute to Free and Open Source software I guarantee you there is a project out there that really needs your help, especially if you are design-minded! Are you into web design? Iconography? Usability? Skinning? UI mockups? I have spoken to many FOSS developers who are not only desperate for this kind of help, but who would also deeply appreciate it and love you to pieces for providing it.

If you encounter some initial resistance when first trying to get started with a project, learn from my experience and do not give up right away. If that project turns out to not be right for you, though, do not worry and move on. Chances are, you are going to find a project you love that loves you back.

2. Help the project help you help them

Many Free and Open Source Software projects today are dominated by programmers and engineers and while some are lucky enough to have the involvement of a creative person or two, for most projects a designer, artist, or other creative's presence is an often-yearned-for-yet-never-realized dream. In other words, even though they understand they need your skills, they may not know what kinds of help they can ask you for, what information they need to give you to be productive, or even the basics of how to work with you effectively.

When I first started getting involved in various FOSS projects, I encountered many developers who had never worked directly with a designer before. At first, I felt pretty useless. I could not follow all of their conversation on IRC because they involved technical details about backend pieces I was not familiar with. When they bothered to pay attention to me, they asked questions like, "What color should I put here?" or "What font should I use?" What I really wanted as an interaction designer was to be privy to decision-making about how to approach the requirements for the project. If a user needed a particular feature, I wanted to have a say in its design – but I did not know when or where those decisions were happening and I felt shut out.

Design contains a pretty wide range of skills (illustration, typography, interaction design, visual design, icon design, graphic design, wordsmithing, etc.) and any given designer likely does not possess all of them. It is understandable, then, that a developer might not be sure what to ask you for. It is not that they are trying to shut you out – they just do not know how you need or want to be involved.

Help them help you. Make it clear to them the kind of work you would like to offer by providing samples of other work you have done. Let them know what you need so they can better understand how to help you engage in their project. For example – when you first get involved in a particular initiative for the project, take the time to outline the design process for it, and post it on the main development list so other contributors can follow along. If you need input at particular points in the process, flag those points in your outline. If you are not sure how particular things happen – such as the process for developing a new feature – approach someone on the side and ask them to walk you through it. If someone asks you to do something beyond your technical ability – working with version-control, for example – and you are not comfortable with that, say so.

Communicating your process and needs will prevent the project from having to make guesses and instead they will be able to make the best use of your talents.

3. Ask questions. Lots of questions. There are no stupid questions.

We have noticed sometimes in Fedora that when new designers come on board, they are afraid to ask technical questions for fear they will look stupid.

The secret is, developers can be so specialized that there are a lot of technical details outside of their immediate expertise that they do not understand either – this happens even within the same project. The difference is that they are not afraid to ask – so you should not be, either! In my interaction design work, for example, I have had to approach multiple folks on the same project to understand how a particular workflow in the software happens, because it is passed off between a number of subsystems and not every person in the project understands how every subsystem works.

If you are not sure what to work on, or you are not sure how to get started, or you are not sure why that thing someone said in chat is so funny – ask. It is a lot more likely someone is going to tell you that they do not know either, than they are going to think that you are stupid. In most cases, you will learn something new that will help make you a better contributor.

It can be especially effective to seek out a mentor – some projects even have mentoring programs – and ask them if they would not mind being your go-to person when you have questions.

4. Share and share often. Even if it is not ready yet. Especially if it is not ready yet.

We have also noticed new designers in Fedora and other Free and Open Source projects are a little shy when it comes to showing their work. I understand that you do not want to ruin your reputation by putting something out there that is not your best or even finished, but a big part of how Free and Open Source projects work is sharing often and openly.

The further along you have come on a piece before you have shared it, the harder others will find it to provide you actionable feedback and to jump in and get involved. It is also harder for others to collaborate on your piece themselves and feel a sense of ownership for it, supporting and championing it through to implementation. In some Free and Open Source projects, not being forthcoming with your sketches, designs, and ideas is even seen as offensive!

Post your ideas, mockups, or designs on the web rather than in email, so it is easy for others in the project to refer to your asset via copying and pasting the URL – especially handy during discussions. The easier it is to find your design assets, the more likely it is they will be used.

Give this tip a try and keep an open mind. Share your work early and often, and make your source files available. You might be pleasantly surprised by what happens!

5. Be as visible as you can within the project community.

One tool that – completely unintentionally – ended up helping me immensely in getting started as a FOSS contributor was my blog. I started keeping a blog, just for myself, as a sort of rough portfolio of the things I had been working on. My blog is a huge asset for me, because:

- As a historical record of project decisions, it is a convenient way to look up old design decisions – figure out why we had decided to drop that screen again, or why a particular approach we had tried before did not work out, for example.

- As a communication device, it helps other contributors associated with your project and even users become aware of what work is happening and aware of upcoming changes in the project. Many times I have missed something essential in a design, and these folks have been very quick to post a comment letting me know!

- It helped me to build my reputation as a FOSS designer, which has helped me build others' trust in my design decisions as time has gone on.

Do you blog? Find out which blog aggregations the members of the project you are working on read, and put in requests to have your blog added to them (there is usually a link to do so in the sidebar.) For example, the main blog aggregator you will want to join to become a part of the Fedora community is called Planet Fedora[1]. Write a first blog post once you have been added introducing yourself and letting folks know what you like – all of the sort of information advised in tip #1.

The project will surely have a mailing list or forum where discussion takes place. Join it, and send an intro there too. When you create assets for the project – no matter how small, no matter how unfinished – blog about them, upload them to the project wiki, tweet/dent about them, and send links to prominent community members on IRC to get their feedback.

Make your work visible, and folks will start to associate you with your work and approach you with cool projects and other opportunities based solely on that.

This is everything I wish I had known when first trying to get involved in Free and Open Source software as a designer. If there is any one thing you should take away from this, it is that you should not be shy – please speak up, please let your needs be known, please let others know about your talents so they can help you apply them to making Free Software rock.

[1] `http://planet.fedoraproject.org`

24. Use of Color and Images in Design Practices

Eugene Trounev

An active member of Free Software and KDE for about 6 years, Eugene Trounev started in KDEGames and followed through the entire KDE3-to-KDE4 transition. Nowadays he is mostly taking care of KDE's web presence and main desktop appearance.

Since the most ancient times people have used the power of images and color to pass information, draw attention, and distract attention. The infamous saying goes "A picture is worth a thousand words", and it could not be more to the point. From the way we dress, to flashy neon light of downtown stores across the globe – every color, every shape and every curve has a purpose.

Knowing the purpose however is not that hard, since all of those variations of hues and lines are put together to be read and felt by every one of us. It is true therefore that a great design must come straight from the heart, as it is supposed to speak to the heart in the first place. Nonetheless, just the heart alone would not be able to make a great design, if some rules are not set and followed at first.

Colors and textures

There are many different ways to classify the colors into categories, but many of them focus on physical or chemical properties of light or ink, and though they are important in the end, those will not help you make an appealing design. The one way that I found works best is to split colors into warm and cool. Simply speaking, warm colors are those closer to the shade of red. They are: red, orange and yellow. Cool colors, on the other end, are the ones running towards blue. They are: green, blue and to a lesser extend violet. It is important to remember that cool is also calm and breathy, while warm is impulsive and dangerous. So, depending on what feelings you wish to awaken within your audience, you should use either warmer or cooler colors. Draw attention with warm and inform with cool. Overuse of either will result in either overheating – creating negative feelings in your viewer, or freezing-over – causing indifference.

It is important to remember that black, white and grays are colors, too. These, however, are neutral. They cause no feeling, but rather set an atmosphere. The properties of these will be discussed later.

Every image is first and foremost a collection of colors, and as such will abide by the rules of color management. Determining the dominant color of your image is the key to success. Try to see the big picture, and do not concentrate on details. A good way to do this is by setting an image against some dark background, then taking a few steps back and observing it from a distance. Which color do you see the most of?

Not all images have a dominant color, however. Sometimes you may come across color bloat, where no matter how hard you look you can not determine which hue dominates. Try to avoid such pictures, as they will inevitably confuse your viewer. When confronted with imagery like that, people tend to look away quickly and it will not give a good impression, no matter what it speaks of.

Beside color, pictures also have a texture, as ultimately they are nothing but a collection of textured colors. Detecting the dominant texture of an image is not as straight forward as its color, as textures are seldom obvious, especially in photographs. There are however a few pointers to help you. Human nature causes us to be drawn to curved, so called "natural" shapes, while angular, sharp-looking shapes are considered less attractive. That is why an image of a curved, green leaf would appeal to more people then that of a metal spike.

To summarize: the key to a successful, appealing design is a good, well balanced combination between color and texture in the images used.

Texts and spaces

An equally important aspect of any good design is the use of text and spaces around it. And just like it is with the image textures and color, you should always remember that people like to breathe. This means that there should be sufficient space in and around the text to make it easier to spot, read and understand.

Consider an example of two pages – one coming from a romantic novel, while the other is taken straight from a legal document. You would most likely prefer the romantic novel over a legal document any day, but do you know why? The answer is simply because you like to breathe. A page from any romantic novel is likely to contain three important elements: a) conversations; b) paragraphs; c) extra wide margins, while most legal documents normally contain neither. All of the aforementioned elements make the page feel alive and dynamic, while the absence of those make it look like a solid wall of text. Human eyes, being more accustomed to a certain degree of variety of sights, feel more at ease when presented with spacious, fluid layouts.

This does not however imply that every text must have all those three elements in order to seem more attractive. Far from it. Any text can be made easy and enjoyable by injecting enough air into the flow.

Air, or space, can come through a variety of ways, such as: letter, line and paragraph spacing; content, section, and page margins; and finally letter size. Try to keep at least one character-toll space between your paragraphs and lines, and two character-toll space between sections in your text. Allow generous spacing around the text on a page by setting your margins wide enough. Try to never go below 10-points font size for your paragraph text, while keeping headings large enough to stand out.

Attraction and information

Just like animals, human beings are often attracted by bright splotches of color and unusual texture, and the more captivating the sight is, the more oblivious people become towards other potential points of interest. This simple rule of attraction has been used since the most ancient times by females and males alike to drive the attention of others away from certain things they did not want to be noticed. The best example of such a trickery is the work of a street magician, who often distracts viewers' attention by use of smoke, flames or flashy attire.

It is important to remember here that words are visual too, as they produce specific associations and visions. The very same trick that can be done with smoke and fires can also be achieved through creative use of wording. By far the best example of a trickery done with words is our every day price tags. Ever wondered why retailers love those .99s and .95s so much? That is because $9.95, or even $9.99 looks more attractive than $10.00, even though in reality they have the same impact on your wallet. Trow an "old" $10.00 price tag noticeably crossed through with a thick red line into the mix and you got yourself a great customer magnet.

Conclusion

Great, attractive design is achieved by following these simple rules: a) choose your imagery wisely; b) make good use of colors and textures to create an atmosphere; c) give your viewer some room to breathe; d) draw the attention away from the parts that matter the least, and towards those that matter the most.

This short essay is not meant to cover the whole wide spectrum of various design styles, techniques and rules, but rather to give you – the reader – a starting point you could carry on building upon.

Part XI.

Community Management

25. How Not to Start a Community

Robert Kaye

Robert Kaye combines his love for music and open source into the open music encyclopedia MusicBrainz. Robert founded and leads the California-based non-profit MetaBrainz Foundation in a long term effort to improve the digital music experience. Beyond hacking on MusicBrainz, Robert seeks out interesting festivals like Burning Man and interesting side projects like hacking on drink-mixing robots. Topped with a colorful hair style at all times, you will never have a hard time picking him out of a crowd.

In 1998, I was working at Xing Technology in San Luis Obispo, working hard on our new AudioCatalyst project. It was one of the first integrated MP3 ripping programs that made use of the CDDB database. CDDB was the CD database that allows any player to look up the title and tracklisting for any CD. If the CD was not listed, you could enter the data so that the next person could make us of the data. I loved this online collaborative project and typed in several hundred CDs over the course of a few years.

One day we were notified that CDDB had been purchased by Escient, a company that would later become GraceNote. The CDDB database was taken private so that people could no longer download the complete database! And on top of that Escient did not compensate any of the contributors for their efforts; they were ripping off the general public with this move. I was quite angry with this move and still am to this day.

A few months later we were notified by Escient that we would be required to play the Escient jingle and display the Escient logo when making a CD lookup in our products. That was it! Now I was livid!

Later that week at a party with friends I was complaining about what was happening and how unhappy I was. My friend Kevin Murphy said to me: "Why don't you start your own open source project to compete with these bastards?"

A few weeks later I stopped working for Xing and had a couple of weeks of spare time before I would start at EMusic. I decided to teach myself Perl and web programming and set out to create the CD Index, a non-compatible, non-infringing project to compete with CDDB. I hacked on the project during the break, but then promptly forgot it once I became a member of the FreeAmp project at EMusic.

Then in March of 1999 Slashdot asked what the open replacement for CDDB was going to be. I spent the rest of that day and most of the night finishing the CD Index and deploying it. I submitted a Slashdot story about my project[1] and it promptly posted. As expected, thousands of geeks showed up within minutes and my server tipped over and died.

The masses of people who arrived immediately started shouting for things to happen. There was not even a mailing list or a bug tracker yet; they insisted on having one right now. Because I was new to open source, I did not really know what all was needed to launch an open source project, so I just did as people asked. The shouting got louder and more people insisted that I shut the service down because it was not perfect. Even amidst the mess, we received over 3000 CD submissions during the first 24 hours.

Once things calmed down, there were still plenty of people shouting. Greg Stein proclaimed that he would write a better version immediately. Mike Oliphant, author of Grip, said he was going to work on a new version as well. Alan Cox came and loudly proclaimed that SQL databases would never scale and that I should use DNS to create a better CD lookup service. Wait, what? I was very unhappy with the community that grew out of the Slashdot posting. I did not want a place were people could treat each other without respect

[1] `http://slashdot.org/story/99/03/09/0923213/OpenSource-Alternative-to-CDDB`

and people who felt entitled could shout louder until they got what they wanted. I quickly lost interest in the project and the CD Index faltered. The other projects that people promised they would start (not counting FreeDB) never materialized.

Then when the dot com bust started, I needed to think about what I would do next. It was clear that my job at EMusic was not safe; still I was driving a Honda S2000 roadster, my dot com trophy car. With car payments double my rent, I had to decide: Work on my own stuff and sell my dream car, or move to the Bay Area and work on someone else's dream, if I could even find a job there.

I decided that a comprehensive music encyclopedia that was user-generated would be the most interesting thing to work on. I sold the S2000 and hunkered down to start working on a new generation of the CD Index. At yet another party, the name MusicBrainz came to me and I registered the domain in the middle of the party. The next day, motivated by the project's new name, I started hacking in earnest and in the Fall of 2000 I launched musicbrainz.org.

Launched is not the right term here – I set up the site quietly and then wondered how I could avoid another Slashdot-based community of loud screaming kids. I never imported data from the CD Index, nor did I mention MusicBrainz on the CD Index mailing lists. I simply walked away from the CD Index; I wanted nothing more to do with it. In the end I decided to add one simple button to the FreeAmp web page that mentioned MusicBrainz.

And a very strange thing happened: people came and checked out the project. It was very few people at first, but when a person mentioned something to me, I would start a conversation and gather as much feedback as I could. I would improve the software based on feedback. I also set a tone of respect on the mailing lists, and every time someone was disrespectful, I would step in and speak up. My efforts directed the focus of the project towards improving the project. I did this for over 3 years before it became clear that this approach was working. The database was growing steadily and the data quality went from abhorrent to good over a number of years. Volunteers come and go, but I am the constant for the project, always setting the tone and direction for the project. Today we have a 501(c)3 non-profit with 3.25 employees in 4 countries, Google, the BBC and Amazon as our customers and we are in the black. I doubt that could have happened with the CD Index community.

I wish I would have known that communities need to grow over time and be nurtured with a lot of care.

26. Hindsight is Almost 20/20

Jono Bacon

Jono Bacon is a community manager, engineering manager, consultant and author. Currently he works as the Ubuntu Community Manager at Canonical, leading a team to grow, inspire and enthuse the global Ubuntu community. He is the author of Art of Community, founder of the Community Leadership Summit and co-founder of the popular podcast LugRadio.

I first learned of Linux and Open Source back in 1998. While the technology was gnarly and the effort required to get a smooth running system was significant, the concept of this global collaborative community transfixed me. Back then I had no knowledge, limited technical skills, and zits.

As an angsty teenager complete with long hair and Iron Maiden t-shirt, my path was really already mapped out for me in the most traditional sense; I would go to school, then college, then university, and then a job.

Fourteen years later, the path I actually took was by no means traditional, and that intrinsic fascination with community has taken me around the world and thrown me into some engrossing challenges. It is interesting to sit back and reflect on this period of time. Well, it might be interesting for me... you might want to skip to the next chapter...

...

Still with me? OK, let's roll.

Science vs. Art

I have always believed that community management is less of a science and more of an art. I define science as exploring methods of reproducing phenomena through clearly understood and definitive steps. In the science world if you know the theory and recipe for an outcome, you can often reproduce that outcome like anyone else.

Art is different. There is no recipe for producing an incredible song, for creating an amazing painting, or sculpting a beautiful statue. Similarly, there is not really any reproducible set of steps for creating a thriving community. Sure, there are tricks and techniques for achieving components of success, but the same happens for other art-forms; we can all learn the notes and chords on a guitar, it does not mean you are going to write the next Bohemian Rhapsody. The formula that generates Bohemian Rhapsody is one part learned skill and one part magic.

Now, I am not suggesting that community management is this frustratingly hip and introverted artform that only the blessed few with such talents can achieve. What I am instead lamenting is that there is no playbook for how to create a wonderful and inspiring community; it is still one part learned skill and one part magic, but the magic part is not divinely anointed to you by the gods, but instead obtained by trying new things, being receptive to feedback, and getting a feel for what works and what does not.

Rather frustratingly, this means that there is no single recipe to follow for the magic, but there is still an opportunity to share the learned skills, as I have sought to do with The Art of Community[1] and the annual Community Leadership Summit[2].

Before I get started reflecting, and for those of you who have not bored yourself into oblivion by following my career, I will summarize the communities I have worked with so we can define the context. In a nutshell, I started out in my hairier days by producing one of the UK's first Linux community websites called Linux UK and got

[1] `http://artofcommunityonline.org`
[2] `http://communityleadershipsummit.com`

involved in the Linux User Group (LUG) community. I went on to create my own LUG in Wolverhampton in the UK and founded the Infopoint project to encourage LUGs to advocate Linux at computer fairs across the UK. I then went on to contribute to the KDE community, founded the KDE::Enterprise site, got the KDE Usability Study going, and contributed to a few little apps here and there. I then founded the PHP West Midlands user group and started also getting interested in GNOME. I wrote a few apps (GNOME iRiver, XAMPP Control Panel, Lernid, Acire) and also co-designed and wrote some code for a new simplified audio app called Jokosher. Around this time I co-founded the LugRadio podcast which would run for four years with over two million downloads and spawning five live events in the UK and USA. At this time I also started work as an Open Source consultant at the government-funded OpenAdvantage where I really got a chance to cut my teeth in community and working with organizations across the West Midlands to help them to move to Open Source. After a few years at OpenAdvantage I moved on to join Canonical as the Ubuntu community manager and developed a team of four and together we are involved in a wide variety of projects in Ubuntu and Canonical.

Still with me?

Wow, you are persistent. Or bored. Probably bored. There will be an exam at the end; that'll learn you...

Reflecting

So this brings me to the focus of this piece – the curious question of if I knew what I did today, what would I tell myself? Over the course of my career so far I believe that everything I have learned can be boiled into two broad buckets:

- Practical – the tips and tricks of the trade; e.g. approaches to communication mediums, using technology in different ways, event planning techniques, project management approaches etc.

- Personal – core life lessons and learnings that affect the approach you take to your world.

I am not going to talk much about the practical – you should read my book for more on that topic (the book also covers a lot of the personal too). Today I am instead going to focus on the personal life lessons. Approaches and practices will always change, but the life lessons do not so much change but grow and evolve as we get wiser.

The Importance Of Belief

Communities are fundamentally networks of people driven by belief. Every community has an ethos and a focus. This could be something as grandiose as documenting all human knowledge or changing the world with Free Software, or it could be as humble as providing a local group for people to get together to talk about their favorite books. Whether life changing or just a bit of fun, each community has a belief system; the humble book club still sees tremendous value in providing a fun, safe and free environment to share reading preferences and recommendations. It might not change the world, but it is still a good thing and something people can get behind.

The underlying often unwritten rule of community is that every contribution from a community member must benefit the wider community. This is why it is fun to write a patch that fixes a Free Software bug, contribute documentation, run a free event or otherwise, but it is rare that anyone is willing to contribute as a volunteer if their contribution only benefits a single person or company.

Of course, I am sure all of you cynical bastards are now going to try and find an exception, but remember that this decision is typically deeply personal – the community member decides how comfortable they are that their contribution will benefit everyone. As an example, some would argue that any contribution to Mono would only benefit Microsoft and the ubiquity of their .NET framework, but hundreds of contributors participate in Mono because they do not see it this way – they see their contributions as a valuable and fun way of making it easy to empower Free Software developers to write Free Software more easily.

If I was talking to the Jono of 1998 I would really emphasize the importance of this belief. I had a hunch about it back then, but I have since seen countless examples of belief truly inspiring people to participate. I have often talked about the story of the kid from Africa who emailed me to tell me how he would walk three hours to and from his nearest Internet cafe to contribute to Ubuntu. He did this because he believed in our mission to bring Free Software to the masses. The same can be said for the tremendous growth in Wikipedia, the incredible coming together of the GNOME community around GNOME 3, the success of OpenStreetMap and many other examples.

Belief though is not a PR stunt. It has to be real. While each of us has different belief systems, some map their belief systems to software, some to education, some to knowledge, some to transparency or whatever else, you can not concoct a belief system unless it serves a valid goal that a group are likely to care about. Sure, it can be obscure, but it has to be real. With the success of Open Source, we have seen some examples of some companies trying to use similar language and approaches around belief, but applying it to self-serving needs. I could invent a belief of "let's all work together to help Jono get rich" and concoct some nonsense of the benefits of this belief (e.g. if I am rich I can focus on other work that would benefit other communities, my future kids would get a wonderful education and upbringing and this will benefit the world), but it would be rubbish.

As such, belief is a strong driver for collaboration and contribution, but it must be met with respect and balance. While it can be a trigger for incredible change, it can also be hugely destructive (e.g. some television preachers who use religion as a means for you to give them money, or fake psychics who use cold reading to latch onto your belief to desperately try and re-connect with a lost loved one).

Your Role

Community managers play an interesting role these days. In the past I have talked about there being two types of community managers; those who go out and give presentations and wave their hands around talking about a product or service, and those who work with a community of volunteers to help them to have a fun, productive and enjoyable collaborative experience. I am more interested in the latter – I feel that is what a real community manager does. The former is a fine and respectable position to have, but it is more in the area of advocacy and public relations, and requires a different set of skills. I have a few tips here I think are interesting enough to share.

The first and probably most important lesson is having a willingness to accept that you can and will be wrong sometimes. In my career so far I have got some things right and some things wrong. While I believe I am generally on the right path and most of my work is successful, there have been a few turkeys here and there. These screw-ups, mishaps and mis-steps have never been out of maliciousness or carelessness, they have instead typically been from me overshooting the target of what I was trying to do.

This seems like a pretty obvious point, but it gets less obvious when you have a fairly public role. By and large, community managers are often seen as representatives of a given community. As an example, I know that I am personally seen as one of the public faces of Ubuntu, and with that responsibility comes the public pressure of how people perceive you.

For some community leaders, having the spotlight shone on them causes a defensive mechanism to kick in; they cringe at the idea of making mistakes in public, as if the chattering masses expect a perfect record. This is risky, and what has been seen in the past is that we get public leaders who essentially never accept that they have made a mistake due to this fear of public ridicule. This is not only a fallacy (we all make mistakes), but it also does not set a good example to the community of a leader who is honest and transparent in both the things they do well and the things they do less well. It is important to remember that we often gain respect in people because of their acceptance of mistakes – it shows a well-rounded and honest individual.

I remember when I first became a manager at Canonical and at the time Colin Watson and Scott James Remnant, two original gangstas from the very beginning of Canonical and Ubuntu, were also managers on the Ubuntu Engineering Team. We would have our weekly calls with our manager, Matt Zimmerman, and on these calls I would hear Colin and Scott openly accepting that they were not good at this, or had made a mistake with that; they were stunningly humble and accepting of their strengths and weaknesses. As a rookie manager I was a little more tight-lipped, but it taught me that this kind of openness and honesty is not only good as a manager but as a community leader and since then I feel no qualms in publicly admitting to mistakes or apologizing if I screw up.

Listening

In a similar way, while openness to mistakes is important, another lesson is the importance of being a good listener and learning from our peers. In many cases our communities look to community managers and leaders as people who should always be providing guidance, direction and active navigation of the project and its goals. This is definitely a responsibility, but in addition to the voicing of this leadership, it is also important to be a passive listener, providing guidance where appropriate and learning new lessons and insight.

Our community members are not just cold, hard, machines who perform work; they are living, breathing, human beings with thoughts, opinions, feelings and ideas. I have seen many examples, and I have accidentally done this before myself, where someone is so used to providing guidance and direction that they sometimes forget to just sit down and listen and learn from someone else's experience. Every industry is filled with thought leaders and scholars ... famous people who are known for their wisdom, but in my experience some of the most revolutionary life lessons that I have learned have come entirely from non-famous, day-to-day, meat-and-potatoes community members. Being a great listener is not just important to help us learn and be better at what we do, but it is critical in gaining respect and having a great relationship with your community.

On vs. Off Time

While on the subject of how we engage with our community, I have another take-away that I only truly processed in my own mind fairly recently. Like many people, I have a number of different interests that fill my days. Outside of being married and trying to be the best husband I can be, and my day job as the Ubuntu Community Manager, I also have projects such as Severed Fifth, the Community Leadership Summit, and some other things. As you would naturally expect, my days are committed to my day job – I do not spend time at work working on these other projects. As such, as you would naturally expect, when my work day ends I start working on these other projects. The lesson here is that it is not always clear to your community where the lines are drawn.

Over the years I have developed a series of online facilities that I use for my work and viewpoints. My Twitter, identi.ca, Facebook pages, my blog, and some other resources are where I talk about what I do. The challenge is that if you take into account these public resources, my public representation of the Ubuntu project, and the wealth of timezones across the world, it does not take an Einstein to confuse whether I am writing about something as a Jono thing or a Canonical thing.

This has caused some confusion. As an example, despite my repeated clarifications, OpenRespect is not and never has been a Canonical initiative. Of course, some idiots choose to ignore my clarification of this, but I can see how the confusion could arrive nonetheless. The same thing has happened for other projects such as Severed Fifth, The Art of Community and the Community Leadership Summit, of which none are, or ever have been, part of my work at Canonical.

The reason why I consider this a lesson is that I have seen, and at one point shared, the view that "of course it is a spare time thing, I posted that at 8pm at night" and shrug of concerns of the lines blurring. When you have a job that puts you in a reasonably public position, you can not have the luxury of just assuming that; you have to instead assume that people are likely to blur the lines and you have to work harder to clarify them.

Don't Travel Too Much

On the topic of working for a company that employs you to be a community leader, you should always be aware of the risks as well as the benefits of travel. This is something I learned fairly early on in my career at Canonical. I would see the same faces over and over again at conferences, and it was clear that these folks had clearly communicated the benefits of travel to their employer, as I had done, but I also came to learn the risks.

I would travel and it would not only be tiring work and emotionally exhausting, but I would also be away from my email more, on IRC less, unable to attend many meetings, and have less time to work on my work commitments. As such, my role would largely become that of getting out and visiting events, and while fun, this did not serve my community as well as it should have done. As such, I fairly dramatically cut my travel – in fact, I went to the Linux Collab Summit a few days ago, and outside of Ubuntu events that I needed to attend, I had not made it to conference for nearly a year. Now I feel the pendulum has swung a little too far in the other direction, so it is all about balance, but I also feel I serve my community better when I am able to take the time to be at the office and be online and accessible.

Planning

For some folks, the role of a community leader or community manager is one that is less about pre-disposed structure and instead more interrupt-driven. When I started out, I used to think this too. While there is absolutely no doubt that you do indeed need to be interrupt-driven and able to respond to things that are going on, it is also essential to sufficiently plan your work for a given period of time.

This planning should be done out in the open where possible and serves a few functions:

- Shares plans – it helps the community to understand what you are working on and often opens up the doors for the community to help you.
- Offers assurances – it demonstrates that a community leader is doing something. Your community can see your active work happening. This is particularly important, as much of the work of a community leader often happens out of the view of the wider community (e.g. having a one-on-one conversation with a community member), and this lack of visibility can sometimes generate concerns that little is happening in key areas, when instead a lot is going on behind the scenes.
- Communicates progress up and down the ladder – this is relevant if you are working for a company. Having some solid planning processes in place demonstrates your active work to your management, and it also re-assures your team that they will always know what to work on and create great value for the community.

Over the years I have put more and more importance in planning, while still retaining enough time and flexibility to be interrupt-driven. When I started as the Ubuntu Community Manager my planning was fairly personal and ad-hoc – I took the pulse of the community, and I applied my time and resources to tend to those areas as I saw fit.

Today I break goals into a set of projects that each span an Ubuntu cycle, gather input from stakeholders, put together a roadmap, track work in blueprints, and assess progress using a variety of tools and processes such as my burndown chart, regular meetings, and more. While the current approach requires more planning, it helps significantly with the benefits covered in the above bullet points.

Perception and Conflict

One thing I often hear about in the world of community management and leadership is the view that perception is everything. Typically when I hear this it is in response to someone getting the wrong end of the stick about something, often in a conflict period.

Of course, perception does indeed play an important part in our lives, but what can fuel incorrect or misaligned perceptions is lack of information, mis-information, and in some cases, heated tensions and tempers. This can be some of the most complex work for a community leader, and I have come away with a few lessons learned in this area too.

Communities are groups of people, and in every group there are often common roles that people fill. There is usually someone who is seen as a rockstar and hero, someone who is sympathetic to concerns and worries and a shoulder to cry on, someone who is overtly outspoken, and often someone who is ... well ... deliberately difficult. Heroes, sympathetic ears and outspoken folks are not particularly challenging, but deliberately difficult people can be complex; if someone is being overtly difficult to deal with, it can cause tensions to form with other members and bring conflict to an otherwise happy community. We need to nip those issues in the bud early.

Part of the challenge here is that people are people, groups are groups, and it is not uncommon for a single person or a few people to become known and complained about behind closed doors as difficult to work with. In addition to this, most people do not want to get involved in any conflict, and as such the person being complained about can sometimes never actually know that people see them this way, as no-one wants to confront them about it. This results in one of the most dangerous situations for a community members – a reputation is spread, without the knowledge of the person who it applies to, and because they never know, they never have an opportunity to fix it. That is a pretty sucky position to be in.

A common response to this conclusion is the view that "they are so difficult to deal with that trying to reason with them will fall on deaf ears anyway". While this certainly does happen from time to time, do not be so quick to assume this will be the outcome; there have been a few times when I have had the uncomfortable experience of feeling I need to share with someone the reputation that they have developed, and in virtually all cases it has been a real surprise to them, and they have almost all modified their behavior based on the feedback.

On a related note, while often not a common part of the daily routine of a community leader, conflict will often raise its head here and there. I just wanted to share two brief elements about conflict.

The first is understanding how conflict forms. To introduce this, let me tell you a little story. Last week a friend of mine flew out to the Bay Area for a conference. He arrived in the evening, so I picked him up from the airport and we went to the pub to catch up. While there he started telling me how disappointed he was with Obama and his administration. He cited examples of health care reform, Wall Street reform, digital rights and more. His agitation was not with the policies themselves, but with Obama not doing enough. My perspective was a little different.

I am not a democrat or a republican; I make my decisions on each issue, and I do not align myself with either party. Where I differ to my friend though is that I am a little more sympathetic to Obama and his daily work. This is because I believe that he, and anyone else in a public position, whether as internationally recognized as the president, or as obscure and specific as a community manager, realizes that the story read and understood by the public is often only a fragment of the full story. There have been cases in the past where something controversial has kicked off in the communities that I have been a part of, and many of the commentators and onlookers have clearly not had a full knowledge of the facts either because they have not picked up on the nuances and details of the topic or some parts of the story have not been shared.

Now, I know what some of you are going to say – some parts not shared?! Surely we should be transparent? Of course we should, and we should always strive to be open and honest, but there are some cases when it would be inappropriate to share some parts of the story. This could be because of private conversations with people who do not want their comments shared, and also just being classy in your work and not throwing dirt around. As an example, I have always had a very strong policy of not throwing cheap shots at competitors, no matter what happens. In the past there has been some questionable behavior from some competitors behind the scenes, but I am not going to go out and throw dirt around as it would not serve a particularly useful purpose, but with that I have to accept that some community critique will only have part of the picture and not be aware of some of the behind the scenes shenanigans.

Finally, on the topic of conflict, I believe a real life lesson I have learned has been the approach in which critique and successful outcomes should be approached. Although blogging has had a hugely positive impact on how people can articulate and share opinions and perspectives, there has been a dark side. Blogging has also become a medium in which much overzealous opinion can sometimes be expressed a little too quickly. Unfortunately, I have a rather embarrassing example of someone who fell into this trap: yours truly.

First, a bit of background. There used to be a company called Lindows that made a version of Linux that shared many visual and operational similarities to Windows. Microsoft frowned at the name "Lindows", and a fight started to change the name. Lindows initially resisted, but after mounting pressure, changed their name to Linspire.

Now to the issue. Let me take the liberty to explain in the words of the article itself:

> Recently a chap named Andrew Betts decided to take the non-free elements out of Linspire and release the free parts as another Linspire-derived distribution called Freespire. This act of re-releasing distributions or code is certainly nothing new and is fully within the ethos of open source. In fact, many of the distributions we use today were derived from existing tools.
>
> Unfortunately, Linspire saw this as a problem and asked for the Freespire name to be changed. Reading through the notice of the change, the language and flow of the words screams marketing to me. I am certainly not insinuating that Betts has been forced into writing the page, or that the Linspire marketing drones have written it and appended his name, but it certainly doesn't sound quite right to me. I would have expected something along the lines of "Freespire has been changed to Squiggle to avoid confusion with the Linspire product", but this is not the case. Instead we are treated to choice marketing cuts such as "To help alleviate any confusion, I contacted Linspire and they made an extremely generous offer to us all". Wow. What is this one-chance-in-a-lifetime-not-sold-in-stores offer? Luckily, he continues, "they want everyone who has been following my project to experience 'the real' Linspire, FOR FREE!!!". Now, pray tell, how do we get this 'real' version of the software "FOR FREE!!!"?
>
> "For a limited time, they are making available a coupon code called 'FREESPIRE' that will give you a free digital copy of Linspire! Please visit `http://linspire.com/freespire` for details". Oh ... thanks.

I gave Linspire a pretty full-throated kick in the wedding vegetables in my blog entry. I told the story, objected to what I considered hypocrisy given their own battle with similar-sounding trademarks, and vented. I wish Guitar Hero had existed back then: it would have been a better use of my time.

I was wrong. My article was never going to achieve anything. Shortly after the article was published, then-CEO Kevin Carmony emailed me. He was not a happy bunny. His objection, and it was valid, was that I flew off the handle without checking in with him first. My blog entry was my first reaction. The reality of the story was far less dramatic, and Linspire were not the ogres that I painted them to be. I apologized to Kevin and felt like an idiot.

Many conflict scenarios are resolved in private discussions where people can be open and focus on solutions without the noise. Over the years I have seen many examples of a furious public blogging war going on while behind the scenes there is a calm exchange of opinions and the focus on solutions.

Wrapping Up

When I started writing this it was much shorter, but I just kept adding one more thing, and then one more thing and so on. It is already long enough that I can probably count the number of people reading this bit on one hand, so I am going to hang it up here. I could go on forever with little tidbits and experiences that I have been fortunate enough to be involved in and expand my horizons, but then I would end up writing The Art of Community II: This Time It's Personal.

Life is a constant on-going experience, and I hope your investment in reading this has added to it a little.

27. Things I'm Happy I Didn't Know

Alexandra Leisse

Alexandra Leisse left one stage to enter another and turn her other passion – software and the web – into a profession. After a transition period of 12 months of freelancing both in software and opera – and sinking countless hours into KDE activities, she joined Nokia, Qt Development Frameworks as Web Community Manager.
She is the woman behind the Qt Developer Network and Qt's community activities on the web. Despite holding a degree in opera performance, she mostly refuses to sing in public.

Introduction

When Lydia asked me to join her book project under the working title of "things I wish I had known", my mind went blank. Things I wish I had known but didn't? Nothing came to mind.

I am not saying that I didn't need to learn anything, on the contrary. I had to learn a lot and I made countless mistakes. But situations or mistakes I would have preferred to avoid? I can't think of any.

All of us have the annoying tendency to look at the things that we could do better, the things we do not know, and perceive them as weaknesses. But what about weaknesses that are our strengths?

Here is my personal story about ignorance, naivety and false perception, and about how happy I am I had no clue.

Names

I had no idea who this guy was I met during the first day of my job. He entered the room, introduced himself, and started asking tough questions that gave me the impression that all I thought I would be doing was nonsense. He was apparently well informed about my doings in KDE and the people I used to deal with. Still we seemed to have different standpoints. At some point I grew tired of his provocations and lost patience. I told him that things are not always as easy with people as engineers wish they were.

It was only after he had left after about an hour of discussing that I googled his name: Matthias Ettrich. What I read explained a lot about why he asked the questions he did. If I had known before that he is one of the founders of the KDE project I would have likely argued in a very different way – if at all.

I had to look up quite some names during the last years, and I was happy every single time that I did it *after* the first contact.

This is probably my most important point. When I met all these FOSS people for the first time I had almost never heard their names before. I did not know about their history, their merits, nor their failures. I approached everyone in the same way: on eye-level.

By being ignorant (or naive, as some have called it), I did not feel inferior to the people I met when I started my journey into FOSS land. I knew I had a lot to learn but I never had the impression I had a lower position than others as a person.

"High-Profile-Project"

I had not religiously followed dot.kde.org nor PlanetKDE, let alone all those countless other FOSS related publications before I started lurking on KDE mailing-lists. I perceived those channels first and foremost as means of communication to a very select audience, mainly users of and contributors to the project itself.

For quite some time, it did not even cross my mind that the articles I published on The Dot might be picked up by journalists. I put an effort into writing them because I wanted to do a good job rather than because I was afraid of making a fool out of myself in the world's face. The press list was maintained by other people and what I wrote did not appear that important to me either. I wanted to reach certain people, and the official channels and my own blog seemed like the most efficient way of doing it.

Being quoted on ReadWriteWeb after announcing on my blog that I would start a new job almost came as a shock to me. It is not that I did not know that people read what I write – I certainly hope they do! – I simply did not expect it to be that much of a topic. It wasn't even summer break.

Good thing nobody told me; I would not have been able to publish a single line.

The Outsider

Some time ago when I attended my first conference I did so with the firm belief that I was different from the other attendees. I saw myself as an outsider because I did not have much in common with anybody else apart from a fuzzy interest in technology: I had been freelancing for some years already after graduating from university, I had no relevant education in the field, and I was mother of a 10 year-old child. On paper at least, it could not get much different from the usual suspects one meets inside FOSS projects.

In 2008 I attended a KOffice sprint as part of the KDE marketing and promotion team to prepare the 2.0 release. The initial idea was to sketch out a series of promotional activities supporting the release to grow both developer and user base, for which there were three of us running a parallel track to the developer discussion.

We tried to understand how we could position KOffice and adapt communication to the intended audience. Pretty soon in the process, we discovered that we had to take a step back: at that point, the immaturity of the suite made it impossible to position it as an option for unsuspecting users. We had to stick with developers and early adopters. It was a tough sell to some of the developers but as outsiders we had the chance to look at the software without thinking of all the blood, sweat and tears that went into the code.

For a lot of projects, no matter of which kind they are, the core contributors have a hard time taking an objective look at the state of affairs. We tend to not see the great accomplishments while we are so focused on the issues in detail, or the other way around. Sometimes we miss a good opportunity because we *think* it has nothing to do with what we are doing – or that no-one would want this in the first place.

In all these cases, people outside the project have the potential to inject some different viewpoints into the discussion, particularly when it comes to prioritization. It is even more helpful if they are not developers themselves: they will ask different questions, will not feel pressured into knowing and understanding all technical details, and they can help decisions and communication on a higher level.

Conclusion

Ignorance is bliss. It is not only true for the individuals who benefits from the fearlessness that results from a lack of knowledge but also for the projects these individuals join. They bring different views and experiences.

And now, go and find yourself a project that interests you, regardless of what you think you know.

Part XII.

Packaging

28. From Beginner to Professional

Jonathan Riddell

Jonathan Riddell is a KDE and Kubuntu developer currently employed by Canonical. When not at a computer he canoes the rivers of Scotland.

There was a bug in the code. A nasty one too: a crash without saving data. That is the problem with looking at code, you find things to fix. It is easy to get involved in Free Software; the difficult part is getting out again. After the first bug fix there are more and more, all within reach. Bug fixes lead to adding features, which leads to project maintenance, which leads to running community.

It started with reading Slashdot, that mass of poorly filtered tech and geek news with comments from anyone who can reload fast enough to get at the top. Every news story was interesting and exciting, a fresh insight into the tech world I was becoming fascinated with. No more did I have to accept what was given to me by large software companies, here in the Free Software community I could see the code develop in front of me.

As a university student it was possible to complete the exercises given by lecturers very quickly, but exercises are not finished programs. I wanted to know how to apply the simple skills they had given me to the real world by writing programs which solve real problems for people. So I looked for the code, which was not hard to find, just lying around on the Internet in fact. Looking closer at the code for the programs I was running I saw beauty. Not because the code was perfectly tidy or well-structured, but because I could understand it with the concepts I had already learned. Those classes, methods and variables fell into place, enabling me to solve the relevant problems. Free Software is the best way to make that step from knowing how to finish exercises in a class to understanding how real programs get written.

Every computing student should work on Free Software for their dissertation. Otherwise you get to spend six months to a year on a project only for it to sit in the basement of a library never to be visited again. Only Free Software makes it possible to excel by doing what comes naturally: wanting to learn how to solve interesting problems. By the end of my project NASA programmers were using my UML diagramming tool and it won awards with lavish receptions. With Free Software you can solve real problems for real users.

The developer community is full of amazing people, with the passion and dedication to work without any more reward than a successful computer program. The user community is also awesome. It is satisfying to know you have helped someone solve a problem, and I appreciate the thank you emails I receive.

Having written useful software, it needs to be made available to the masses. Source code is not going to work for most people, it needs to be packaged up. Before I was involved in it I looked down on packaging as a lazy way to contribute to Free Software. You get to take much of the credit without having to code anything. This is somewhat unfair, much of the community management needed to run any Free Software project can also be seen as taking the credit without doing the code.

Users depend on packagers a lot. It needs to be both fast, to keep those who want the latest and greatest, and it needs to be reliable, for those who want stability (which is everyone). The tricky part is that it involves working with other people's software, and other people's software is always broken. Once software is out in the wild problems start to emerge that were not visible on the author's own computer. Maybe the code does not compile with a different compiler version, maybe the licensing is unclear so it can not be copied, maybe the versioning is inconsistent so minor updates might be incompatible, screen sizes might be different, desktop environments can affect it, sometimes necessary third party libraries do not even have a release. These days software needs to run on different architectures, 64-bit processors caused problems when they became widely available, these days it is ARM which is defeating coders' assumptions. Packagers need to deal with all of these issues, to give something to the users which reliably works.

We have a policy in Ubuntu that packages with unit tests must have those tests enabled as part of the package build process. Very often they fail and we get told by the software author that the tests are only for his or her own use. Unfortunately it is never reliable enough in software to test it yourself, it needs others to test it too. One test is rarely enough, it needs a multi-layered approach. The unit tests from the original program should be the first place to start, then the packager tests it on his or her own computer, then it needs others to test it too. Automatic install and upgrade testing can be scripted on cloud computing services quite nicely. Putting it into the development distribution archive gets wider testing before finally some months later it gets released to the masses. At each stage problems can and will be found which need to be fixed, then those fixes need testing. So there might not be much coding involved but there is a lot of work to get the software from being 95% to being 100% ready, that 5% is the hardest part, a slow and delicate process needing careful attention all the way.

You can not do packaging without good communication with your upstream developers. When bugs happen it is vital to be able to find the right person to talk to quickly. It is important to get to know them well as friends and colleagues. Conferences are vital for this as meeting someone gives much more context to a mailing list post than a year of emails can.

One of the unspoken parts of the Free Software world is the secret IRC channels used by core members of a project. All big projects have them, somewhere out there Linus Torvalds has a way of chatting to Andrew Morton et al about what is good and what is bad in Linux. They are more social than technical and when overused can be very anti-social for the community at large, but for those times when there is a need for a quick communication channel without noise they work well.

Blogging is another important method of communication in the Free Software community. It is our main method of marketing and promotion for both the software we produce and ourselves. Not to be used for shameless self-publicity, there is no point claiming you will save lives with your blog, but used to talk about your work on Free Software it builds community. It can even get you a job or recognized in the street.

Those Slashdot stories of new technology developments are not about remote figures you never meet in the way newspaper stories are. They are about people who found a problem and solved it using the computer in front of them. For a few years I was editing the KDE news site, finding the people who were solving problems, creating novel ideas and doing the slow slog of getting the software up to high enough quality, then telling the world about them. There were never a shortage of people and stories to tell the world about.

My last piece of advise is to stay varied. There is such a wealth of interesting projects out there to explore, learn from and grow, but once in a position of responsibility it can be tempting to stay there. Having helped create a community for Kubuntu I am moving temporarily to work on Bazaar, a very different project with a focus on developers rather than non-tech users. I can start again learning how code turns into useful reality, how a community interacts, how quality is maintained. It will be a fun challenge and I am looking forward to it.

29. Packaging - Providing a Great Route into Free Software

Thom May

Thom May is a Debian Developer, an emeritus Member of the Apache Software Foundation and was one of the first hires for Canonical, Ubuntu's parent company. He currently lives in London and is Head of DevOps for Macmillan Digital Science.

Introduction

I started out in Free Software over a decade ago. I had been using Debian for some years through university, and decided that I wanted to give something back. So I started the long journey through the Debian New Maintainer's process, never having really contributed to Free Software before, and concerned that a lack of experience with C would prove to be a major problem.

As it turned out, this concern was mostly unfounded. By starting out working with packages that I used regularly I was able to contribute effectively. As my experience with the myriad of tools and systems that Debian provides to its maintainers grew, I became more efficient with my time, and was able to take on a wider range of packages.

Taking on more packages increased my exposure to a range of build systems, programming languages and toolkits, and also helped to bring me into the Debian community. Abrasive and opinionated though it is, Debian's community of skilled and experienced maintainers is one of the main reasons Debian has maintained its technical excellence over such a long period.

At about this time the Apache httpd project was finally closing in on the first beta releases of httpd 2.0, which had been several years in the making and was going to be a massive upgrade. Debian's Apache team had been fairly inactive for some time – the 1.3 packages were stable and changed infrequently – and had no plans for packaging 2.0. I had a strong interest in ensuring that the httpd packages were well maintained – I was working as a sysadmin in charge of numerous Apache web servers – so it made a lot of sense to take on the challenge of producing packages for the new release.

A friend and I started work on the packages and quickly discovered that while the code was approaching an early beta quality, the tooling around the build and customization of httpd was sadly lacking, which is fairly typical for many complex software projects.

Over the course of the best part of a year – whilst upstream stabilised their code and an increasing number of early adopters began to test and deploy the new release – we worked hard to ensure that the build system was sufficiently flexible and robust to cope with the stringent requirements of Debian's policy. As well as ensuring that our packages were technically correct, we had to ensure that our relationship with upstream allowed us to get patches back upstream whenever possible, and to get a heads up whenever security issues arose and for early testing of release candidates.

My interactions with Apache in the course of packaging and maintaining httpd 2.0 led me to become an upstream committer on the project, meaning I could contribute code directly. This is generally the final step in moving from packaging software to actively developing it for a wider audience than your distribution. On a personal level, this recognition gave me the confidence to contribute to far more Free Software projects, since I knew that my code was of sufficient quality to be welcomed.

Evolution - from packager to developer

So how did this happen? Packaging in its simplest form ensures that a given software project complies with the policy of the distribution; in my case Debian. Generally, this means configuring the software at build time so that files are placed in the correct directory locations (specified by the File Hierarchy Standard, or FHS), that dependencies on other packages are correctly specified, and that the software runs successfully on the distribution.

More complex packaging can require splitting an upstream project into multiple packages, for example libraries and the header files that allow the user to compile software against that library are shipped in separate packages, and platform dependent files can be shipped separately from platform independent ones. Ensuring that the upstream software correctly deploys in these situations will often require changes to the code. These changes are the first step into active work on a project, rather than the sometimes passive act of packaging.

Once your package is available in the distribution it is exposed to millions of potential users. These users are guaranteed to run your software in ways that neither you, as packager, nor your upstream expected. Unsurprisingly, with many eyes come many bug reports. Debian, in common with most distributions, encourages its users to submit bug reports directly to Debian, rather than to the individual upstream projects. This allows maintainers to triage bug reports and ensure that the changes made during the packaging process are not the cause of the reported problem. Often there can be considerable interaction between the reporter of the problem and the package maintainer before the upstream developers become involved.

As the package maintainer increases their knowledge of the project, they will be able to solve most problems directly. The maintainer will often release bug fixes directly into Debian in parallel with feeding them back upstream, allowing for swift problem resolution and considerable testing of fixes. Once a fix is confirmed the maintainer will then work with the upstream project to ensure that the required changes happen in the upstream, definitive project, so that they are available to other users of the software.

Providing successful bug fixes on distributions such as Debian is often a complex art form. Debian runs on many platforms, from IBM mainframes to smart phones, and the range and breadth of these platform swiftly reveals assumptions in the code. More often than not the packager has easier access to a broader range of platforms than upstream does, and so is the first port of call when a knotty porting problem does come up. One quickly learns to recognise the symptoms of pointer size assumptions, endianness problems, and many other esoteric issues; this experience makes one a more versatile and cautious programmer.

As a package collects bug fixes and improvements, it is essential to feed those changes back upstream. Too often the delta between a package and the definitive, upstream software can grow enormously, with the effect that the two become almost entirely separate code bases. Not only does this increase the maintenance burden on both sides, but it can cause huge frustration and waste large amounts of time for your upstream should a user of your package report a bug related to one of the changes in the packaged version to the upstream. To this end, a close working relationship with upstream and an understanding of the best way for both parties to collaborate is vital.

Collaboration between upstream and packager can take many forms. Whether it be finding the correct way to communicate bug reports, making sure you use the correct coding style, or ensuring that you both use the same version control system in the same way, making sure that your interactions are as friction-free as possible, makes for a far better relationship with upstream and a greatly increased likelihood that your upstream will take the time to help you when you need it.

Once the working relationship between you and your upstream is established, it becomes an easy step to contribute more directly to upstream. This, too, can take many forms. Simple first steps can involve synchronising any upstream bug reports with the ones from your distribution, making sure that duplicate effort is not expended to root cause and fix bugs. More direct involvement entails feature development and changes with a wider scope than would be palatable when made in a packaged version.

Conclusion

I think the two core things I wish I had known when starting out are the sense of community that Free Software engenders, and the fantastic route that packaging of Free Software provides into the wider Free Software world.

Community is critical to the success of Free Software. It comes in many forms, from the legion of users willing to invest time in making your software better, to one's peers in a distribution or software project who invest their time and energy into honing your skills and ensuring that your contributions are as good as possible.

The route from packaging into development is one often traveled. It provides a learning curve less steep than entering a development community cold, and allows one to develop skills at a more gradual rate than would otherwise be the case.

30. Where Upstream and Downstream Meet

Vincent Untz

Vincent Untz is an active Free Software enthusiast, GNOME lover and advocate, as well as an openSUSE booster. He held the position of GNOME Release Manager between 2008 and 2011, until GNOME 3.0 went out, was an active GNOME Foundation director (2006-2010) and is leading the GNOME team in openSUSE. However, he finds it simpler to declare he is a "touche-à-tout", working on various (some say random) areas of the desktop and helping openSUSE stay amazing. Vincent is still pushing French as official language for GNOME, and hopes to succeed really soon now. And he loves ice cream.

A long time ago, in a room at night...

I took a last look at the list of bugs to see if I had not forgotten a patch that should be merged. I made sure to write what I thought was a descriptive `NEWS` entry about the new version. I typed `make distcheck` to start the release process and looked at the terminal display hundreds of lines. A tarball got created, and I double-checked that the tarball was building fine. Again and again – I was anxious and somehow did not fully trust the `make distcheck` command. After checking everything several times, I uploaded the tarball to the server and sent a mail announcement.

I had managed to do it: I had released my first tarball of a software of which I had recently become co-maintainer. And I was certainly thinking: "now users can enjoy some goodness!" But mere seconds after my tarball got uploaded, a few people downloaded it and made my release really accessible to users.

This is something I took for granted, as I thought it was mostly a trivial task. I thought wrong.

Upstream Versus Downstream

As users, we do not necessarily understand the different steps required to ship software to us. It is here, and we can simply enjoy it.

Many people contribute to this process of shipping software, and the effort is usually split between two groups of people, which are central in how Free Software works today:

- **upstream**: This is the group creating the software. It obviously includes coders, but depending on the project, other categories of contributors also are key participants: designers, translators, documenters, testers, bug triagers, etc. Upstream generally only ships the source code in a compressed archive, a tarball.

- **downstream**: This is the group responsible for distributing the software to the users. In the very same way as for upstream, contributors have a wide range of profiles, as they work on translations, documentation, testing, bug triage and more. There is however a profile that is, as of now, unique to downstream: the packagers, who prepare the software to make it available in a format suitable for easier use than just source code, a package.

Interestingly, this is a rather intuitive split for users too, although we are unaware of it: we often assume that the software developers are unreachable, and we send feedback and ask for help to the distributors instead.

A concrete analogy to clarify this upstream–downstream split could be the usual model for physical goods, with retail stores ($\approx$ downstream) distributing products of manufacturers ($\approx$ upstream), and playing an important role for customers ($\approx$ users).

A Closer Look at Downstream

If I had to summarize in one sentence the role of downstream, this is how I would describe it:

> Downstream is the bridge between users and upstream.

When I released my first upstream tarball, I was assuming that for downstream, the work would mostly be compiling the source and building a package out of it, and nothing else. Building a package is indeed the first step, but this is only the beginning of the journey for downstream: then come several different tasks, some of which are purely technical while others are social. I will only very briefly describe this journey here, in a non-exhaustive way, as this could be a whole part of this book[1].

The building of the package itself can be less trivial than expected: it is not uncommon that the packager hits some issues that were unknown to upstream, like when a new version of the compiler is used (with new errors), or a specific library needs to be updated first (because the tarball is using some new API), or the build system of the tarball is tailored for a specific way of working (which does not follow the guidelines of the targetted distribution). What is even more ignored by many is that all those issues can also occur after the tarball has already been packaged, like when migrating the whole distribution to a new compiler or toolchain. None of those technical issues are extremely difficult to handle per se, and upstream is often happy to help solve them; but without downstream, those issues could go unnoticed by upstream for a while.

[1] It is worth mentioning that I do not believe that downstream should significantly modify the software released by upstream; some downstreams do that, however, and this adds to their workload.

What is more important to me than those technical challenges is that downstream is generally in direct contact with more users than upstream. This results in bug reports, support requests, requests to change configuration defaults, and more. This is where the downstream crowd really shines: instead of simply forwarding all of this upstream, downstream will work on this feedback from users to only relay summarized bits that upstream will be able to use. Often, bug reports come without enough information on the issue (in which case downstream will ask for more details); often, the support requests stem from a misunderstanding on the user side (which downstream can then, sometimes, translate to a suggestion to change the software to avoid such misunderstanding); often, new configuration defaults are suggested without a good-enough rationale (and downstream will work with the users to see if there is a valid rationale). Of this huge amount of data, downstream will produce a smaller set of information that upstream will be able to easily consume, which will lead to improvements in the software.

There are generally two rewards for downstream contributors: the indirect and direct contributions to the upstream project thanks to the efforts done downstream are enough for many, but on top of that, the direct contact with more users leads to being exposed to the satisfaction of those users. And such exposure easily makes a day for many people.

As a sidenote, when considering the amount of work involved downstream, I would not be surprised if, at the end of the day, many upstream contributors are glad to have downstream people act as a buffer to them: this significantly lowers the amount of feedback, while at the same time improving the quality of the feedback (by avoiding duplicated comments, undetailed issues, etc.). This enables upstream to stay focused on the development itself, instead of forcing upstream to either triage feedback or ignore it.

Just looking at my own upstream experience, I cannot count the number of patches I received from downstream to fix build issues. I also remember countless discussions about the bugs that were affecting users the most, that helped me organize my priorities. And since I joined the downstream ranks, I started sending similar build-related patches to upstream, and chatting with my downstream hat to relay feedback from users. Such upstream–downstream collaboration contributes to improving the overall quality of our Free Software ecosystem, and I would consider it essential to our good health.

Pushing Downstream Upstream!

I am firmly believing that there must be a strong upstream–downstream collaboration for a project to succeed. I doubt there is much disagreement on this by anyone; however, by "downstream", people usually think of the work being done in distributions. But, especially, for applications, it is becoming more and more viable to push that downstream work out of distributions and to get benefits from such a move upstream.

Tools like the Open Build Service make it easy to have people build and distribute packages of an application for several distributions. This has benefits for both the users (who can more easily and more quickly enjoy updates of their favorite applications) and for upstream (who can help build a stronger relationship with its user base). The only challenge with such a move is that there still needs to be someone doing the packaging work, but also to manage the larger feedback from users. That is, there still needs to be someone doing the downstream work; except that it would be done as part of upstream.

To me, this sounds like an exciting perspective, and I would even go as far as suggesting that we, the Free Software community, should slowly migrate the downstream work being done in distributions to be based on downstream work being done directly upstream whenever possible – and at least for applications, this is often possible. This obviously requires a mind shift, but it would allow more sharing of the efforts that are most of the time being duplicated in all the different downstreams as of today.

For people willing to start contributing nowadays to applications they like, this packaging work upstream is a whole new approach that could be really successful!

I tried it and I stayed, will you?

Downstream has always been essential to my life as a Free Software user – after all, only a few people are manually building their whole system from scratch and I am not one of them. But it also became an asset to me as an upstream developer, as I started taking more time to discuss with downstream people to get more feedback on bugs, features, general quality and even future directions of the software I was working on.

This is only when I started being a downstream myself that I understood that this position is indeed a privileged one to help advise upstream, because of the direct contact to users and because of the different perspective we get from this different position.

Without downstream, we would not be where we are today. If you want to make a difference, be sure that by joining a downstream effort and talking to upstream, you will succeed.

And you will have fun.

Part XIII.

Promotion

31. Finding Your Feet in a Free Software Promotion Team

Stuart Jarvis

Stuart Jarvis began working with the KDE Promotion Team in 2008 by writing articles for KDE's news website, KDE.News. He learned the hard way how to get things done in a free software community and got more involved with promotion team activities such as writing KDE's release announcements and getting articles about KDE software into the Linux press. He now sits on KDE's Marketing Working Group, helping to set the direction of KDE's promotion and marketing activities and helping new contributors to find their feet. He is also now part of the editorial team for KDE.News, where his involvement with KDE first began.

"He who codes, decides" is the mantra of free software development. But what if there is no code? Or the he is a she?

Joining the promotion and marketing team of your favorite free software project presents some special challenges. For new coders, most projects have code review systems, maintainers and pre-releases of software that all help to spot errors in code, making contributing your first patches less scary.

Promotion can require your work to be visible to the public, with minimal review, almost immediately. The non-hierarchical nature of free software communities means there often is not a single person you can turn to who will tell you whether your ideas are right and take some of the responsibility on your behalf.

Getting consensus versus getting it done

I first started contributing to KDE by writing articles for the official news site, KDE.News. I had written for news outlets before, but always had a named person to whom I would send a draft, receive feedback and then make changes as required. In the KDE promotion team there was no single person or group of people "in charge". I had to try and gauge the responses I got to draft articles and decide whether I had all the feedback I needed and the article was ready for publication.

With guidance from more experienced contributors, I eventually learned how to propose something and get it published within a few days if there were no major objections. The approach can be used by any contributor to a free Software Promotion team, new or old alike.

First, work out how you would do something, whether it be writing an article, changing a website text or giving a talk at your local school. Make a plan or write the article or the new text. Send your ideas for review on the promotion team mailing list of your organization. Importantly, do not ask people what they think – you can wait for days or weeks and not get definite answers. Instead, state that you will publish or submit your text or execute your plan by a set date in the future, pending any objections in the meantime.

When setting a deadline for comments, think about how long it will take everyone active in the team to check email and consider your proposal. Twenty-four hours is likely the absolute minimum for a simple yes or no answer to a straightforward question. For something that requires reading or research, you should allow several days.

If there are no big objections within the time limit you set, you can just go ahead. If there are big problems with your plan, someone will tell you. Things actually get done, you do not get frustrated with a lack of progress and you get a reputation for completing tasks successfully.

Ultimately, it is your decision

Free software communities can easily become discussion groups. Everyone has an opinion. If you are not careful, discussions can become large, fade away as people lose interest and finish without reaching any strong conclusions. That can be hard enough to deal with when you have been around the community for a while and have the experience to make your own decisions and your own views on whose opinions you should listen to. When you are just starting out, it can be very confusing.

If you want your own task to succeed, you may have to make decisions between competing view points. You can wrap up the discussion by providing a summary of the main points made and stating your opinion on them. Try not to leave any open questions unless you want further discussion – just state your conclusions and what you are going to do. As long as you are reasonable, people are likely to respect you even if they disagree.

Be proactive – do not wait to be asked

Your first contact with the promotion team you want to join may well be by sending an email to their mailing list offering your skills. I thought I could list things I was good at and expect people to suggest things for me to do. Normally, it does not work quite like that.

Most communities are short of volunteers and really do need your skills. However, because they lack volunteers, they can also lack time to provide good guidance and mentoring. If there is a specific short-term project you would like to work on, say so. It is much easier for someone in the project to simply say "go ahead" than to try and come up with a project to match your skills.

Even when you have worked on a few projects and proven your skills, you are unlikely to often be approached personally with tasks. Those coordinating the marketing team will not know your personal circumstances and so might not feel comfortable asking you to do something specific in your own time, for free. An ideal community will regularly post – either on a mailing list or a web page – tasks that volunteers can pick up. If that does not happen, find your own things to do and tell the mailing list that you are doing them. People will notice and it raises the chance that you will be directly approached in the future.

If you are proactive then you can quickly find that you are one of the experienced people in the community that new people look to for advice and jobs to work on. Try and remember what it was like when you started and make their lives as new contributors as easy as possible.

32. Big Plans Don't Work

Jos Poortvliet

Jos Poortvliet works as openSUSE community manager for SUSE Linux. Before that he was active in the international KDE community as team lead for the marketing team. In his "offline life" he has had jobs at a variety of companies as Business Consultant. His favorite pastime is experimenting in the kitchen, trying to come up with something edible.

> "It is better to take many small steps in the right direction than to make a great leap forward only to stumble backward." – Old Chinese proverb

A great idea...

Once upon a time in the marketing team of a Free Software project, someone came up with a great idea to grow the project. A program would be set up to get IT students to learn about the project and join in. Universities would be contacted and someone would talk to them to get them interested. Ambassadors would then go to those universities and give a course there, coaching students in their first step into the world of Free Software. Once they joined online, they would be mentored on simple tasks and finally become full-fledged contributors! Of course, universities would love the program, and with some luck start to participate more actively, giving their students assignments which result in code being written for the project, and much more.

... which didn't work...

I have seen the idea from the fictitious story above in many forms in many different communities and projects. It is a great idea and could be very powerful! We all know you have to start early – our proprietary competition is pretty darn good at this. We also know we have arguments enough to convince universities and students to participate – FOSS is the future, it provides great skill development opportunities, skills in Linux programming or administration are in higher demand than another Java or .NET developer or Windows sysadmin and most importantly: it is more fun. Somehow, however, if you go to universities, you do not see many posters inviting you to join Free Software projects. Most professors have never heard of it. What went wrong? Let me continue the story.

... not because lack of effort...

The team had a long discussion about it. First brainstorm style – many ideas on how to realize the idea came in. The team leader collected the work and put it on the wiki. A plan was made with a time line and the team leader appointed people responsible for certain parts. Some started writing course materials, others looked up university contact information and put it in a list. They asked frequently for input and ideas on the mailing list and got plenty of responses for further course material, which the leader added to the list of things to write. It all had to be done in the free time of the volunteers, but you could always count on the leader to remind volunteers of the schedule.

After a few months a structure was visible and many pages in the wiki were created. Meanwhile, however, the number of people involved decreased from the initial discussion with over 30 to about 5 still soldiering on. The leader decided to revise the road map with proposed deadlines and after a few calls on the mailing list 10 new volunteers committed to a variety of tasks. The pace picked up a bit again. Quite a bit of what had been done before had to be updated and there were other adjustments needed. Unfortunately, things kept slipping and the number of people doing things kept decreasing. Monthly sprints were introduced which did indeed result in some more work being finished. But there was simply too much to do. After about a year, the last people gave up. A stale wiki page and some outdated materials are all that is left...

... but because it was too ambitious.

So why did it not work? They team did everything according to the best project management practices you will find on the web... brainstorming, then creating a plan, time lines, clear goals and responsibilities... They did the right volunteer things: ask people, engage them, give everyone an opportunity to voice his/her opinion. It should have worked!

It did not, because of a simple reason: it was too ambitious. It is a trend. Amazing ideas receive lots of comments, get written down in great plans which result in incomplete wiki pages leading to too little implementation finally fading into nothingness.

Leaders have to recognize that how a team works in FOSS is not the same as in a structured, managed environment like a company. People tend to be around when there is something exciting, like a big release, and then disappear until the next exciting thing. Creating a community team should never assume that the people will stay fully committed the entire length of time. You have to factor in that they will be in for a while and then disappear for longer periods and then come back. The leaving and joining creates a lot of overhead so that little gets done. Yes, we can lead people, but we cannot manage people, and once you learn to give up the management aspect, you can focus more on things you need to do in the immediate short term.

So instead of planning big things, find something small, doable and useful in itself. Not a wiki page with a plan, but the first step of what you aim for. And then, lead by doing. Make a rough first draft of an article. Make a first version of a folder. Copy-paste from whatever exists, or improve something which was already available. Then present the result, drafty as it is, to the team and ask if someone wants to make it better. Do something small and it will work.

Don't plan, just do...

So how do you do something as big as the university student plan? You don't! At least, not directly. Discussing this with the whole team, planning – it will surely make for a fun discussion which can last weeks. But it will not get you far. Instead, keep the plan to yourself. Seriously.

I am not saying that you should not talk about it – you can. Share the ambition with whoever is interested. And it is OK if they give suggestions. But do not rely on it, do not make plans which go much further than the first 1-2 steps. Instead, execute. Build on what is there. Send a draft of a new or improved flyer to the mailing list. Ask someone who gave a course on your project to share the material and improve it a bit. Those whose work you build on might help you out! The people you spoke with about the plan who share your vision might help you too. This way, you will frequently finish something – a flyer, an improved website, a presentation to be used. And people can, slowly, start using it. Ambassadors can go to their local universities, using a few of the things you have already created. To do what they do, they surely have to create some missing materials – which can go on the wiki as well. And you make progress.

... and get your pie in the sky!

In community marketing, strategy is not on the wiki. It is not in a plan nor a time line. Neither is it discussed every week with the whole team. It is part of a vision which has grown over time. It is carried by a few central people and inspires the short-term plans and objectives. And it is shared by the team. But it has no time line and it can not fail. It is flexible and does not depend on anything or anyone in particular. And it will always be a pie in the sky...

So if you want to lead in a Free Software community marketing effort, keep that big picture a big picture. Do not plan too much, but get things done!

33. Who are You, What are You Selling, and Why Should I Care?

Sally Khudairi

Active in the Web since 1993, Sally Khudairi is the publicist behind some of the industry's most prominent standards and organizations. The former deputy to Sir Tim Berners-Lee and long-time champion of collaborative innovation, she helped launch The Apache Software Foundation in 1999, and was elected its first female and non-technical member. Sally is Vice President of Marketing and Publicity for The Apache Software Foundation, and Chief Executive of luxury brand communications consultancy HALO Worldwide.

Everyone is a marketer. From the CEO to the superstar salesperson to the guy in the mailroom, everyone is a representative of your company. Technologies and tactics have changed over the years but good communications remain paramount. At the end of the day, everyone is selling something, and it is an interesting balance in publicity, as who and what you are and what you sell are often enmeshed. When people tell me that they do not know who I am, I ask if they have heard of W3C, Apache, or Creative Commons. The typical reply is "of course", which assures me that I am doing my job. If you know who and what *they* are, things are good. It is about the product, not the publicist, after all. I never set out to be in this space: cutting my communications teeth during the nascent web years was not easy, but I am grateful to have had the opportunity to observe others and dodge quite a few bullets. A sharp ramp-up and some very highly-visible projects later, what advice would I share with a budding PR bunny, seasoned media flack, or technologist daring to ride the promotions bucking bronco?

Never forget to declare yourself

In selling your story to the press, remember that the media, too, have something to sell. Sure, at the top level the role of a journalist is to tell a compelling story (truthfully or not, factually or not, ethically or not, is another issue). From attracting readership to securing subscriptions to promoting ad space, they too are selling something, and your job is to help them do their job. The reality is that some folks may not have heard of you, even if you have been around for a long time. Or even if they have, they may not know who you are exactly. Be clear with what it is that you have to offer. What is the press hook – what is the news? Be sure that the news is *really* news. Be direct and get to the point quickly. You have got to be prepared to answer the questions: "So what?" "Why should I care?" "What is in it for me?", and that means having to ask questions of yourself and your product. People buy ideas, not products, so promoting the benefits of what you are pitching will help improve your chances of securing coverage. Spin aside, what are you really selling?

Never on a Friday

The worst day to launch a new website, issue a press release, or brief the media is on a Friday. The chance that something wrong will happen with nobody available to deal with the fallout is greater than you can imagine. A poignant reminder of this happened to me early in my career when I launched the new W3C homepage on a Friday evening, left the office and boarded a plane for Paris. Coming from the world of commercial web publishing, using a proprietary tag was not an issue whatsoever as long as it got the job done. Doing so on the website of an interoperability-all-the-way organization on the other hand was Not A Good Thing. Within minutes dozens of messages were pouring in, wondering how the <now-deprecated-markup>-tag got on our site. And no, it was not <blink>...

Never think that it doesn't matter

Credibility is everything. Despite being overworked, overcommitted or overextended, you can not un-strike a bell. Try to deliver as much as you can to the best of your ability and ask for help if you can. Some deadlines have to be adjusted, and many editors can accommodate shift in schedule but it likely will not matter (as much) once the story/fire has gone out if you are unable to follow through. Like art, standards development, and copywriting, the process can go on ad nauseam. Whilst creativity can not be time-managed, hard deadlines force a line to be drawn at some point. But you have got to care about the details. Stop. Proof-read and check all links. Make sure it maps properly to the overall campaign/brand strategy. Lather-rinse-repeat is part of the greater communications gestalt, and the work will keep piling up. Sort it out and protect your reputation.

Do go at it alone

It is important to trust your instincts, particularly when doing something separate from the norm. In the early days of that newfangled web thaang, everyone was seemingly tacking on the usual branding/PR/marketing tactics to a brochure-ware Website. Then everyone was "following the leader" (leader = "whoever did it first" in many instances). Trends are one thing, industry expectations and requirements are another: "that is how everybody does it" does not mean that it is right for you, your project or community. My career in communications began when I fired our retained agency and brought everything in-house. We were one of the earliest organizations to use a URL in a corporate boilerplate, and were the first to use a URL as the originating location on a press release dateline despite news wire agencies telling it was non-conformant and against policy. Stand confidently in your knowledge. Go against the grain and challenge the rules responsibly. Individuate. It is OK to be a dissenter as long as you can back your ideas up.

Do provide perspective

Many of the technologies I am involved with wind up in products 3-5 years down the road. This means that, in many instances, it is hard to establish some sort of relationship to a comparable product. It is critical that you explain your position clearly with as little jargon as possible. Most non-developer journalists/analysts I deal with do not follow the day-to-day activities of a certain community or know the technical ins-and-outs of why one feature is better than another, no matter how much of a no-brainer it is to you. The saying of "sell the sizzle, not the steak" is more relevant today than ever. Sizzle. Steak. There is always a split on this when I teach media training: provide too much steak or too much sizzle and your campaign could fail. Perception is key and the cause of a lot of conflict: All Sizzle = "hype + hyperbole" = "oh, you PR types". All Steak = "0s and 1s" = "oh you geek types". You need to understand and be able to clearly explain the painpoint that your product solves. Knowing how to better present the problem allows you to better explain the solution. Context, anecdotes, and success stories give the press a way to make their readers care. You have got to know the answer to the question "What is in it for me?", because that is what incents journalists to delve deeper into your story, which, in turn, gets readers to learn more about you. Sizzle answers "What's in it for me?", and is therefore the hook. Steak is *how* you get there.

Do queue up your spokespeople

Always have someone available to talk to the press. Yes, it can be you, but know that there will be a time that although you have a well-planned story to tell, you may not be available to tell it. Who else do you work with? Who knows you? Who endorses you? Defining those individuals and making a message map that clarifies who says what helps alleviate an awful lot of potential headaches. I usually act as the "backgrounder" spokesperson so I can spend time with a reporter to find out what specifically are they looking for and how can we best provide them with relevant information. I explain how things work, mostly process-oriented; this puts my "actual" spokespeople in a better position to say what they need, and minimize the risk of having their participation getting lost elsewhere. Getting the right people ready is just as important as making them available. In my media training classes, I include some "Yikes!" slides that highlight particularly interesting lessons learned over the years. For example, we experienced spokesperson mayhem in the early days of the Apache Incubator, where 15 people responded to a press query in 48 hours ... lots of opinions, but who was the "right" one to quote? Do not leave it to the press to decide! Another oft-shared "Yikes!" scenario involved a global launch party with hundreds of guests, press everywhere, DJs spinning, music blaring, cocktails flowing, and the event running very late into the night, with rumored spin-off after-parties. Very early the following morning the press queries came in (yes, of course I will accept a phone call from the Financial Times at 4AM PT!). I pitched excitedly. However, it turned out that we had no spokespeople available: Chairman on a plane to Japan; Director's mobile phone was off (with reason, apparently); Board members unavailable; staff unprepared. Dozens of opportunities missed. Remember: when the press release goes out on the wire, the work has just begun.

Don't be surprised to take it from all sides

Everyone has an opinion. And they will likely give it to you.

Don't overcomplicate things

If you think you have got too much to tell, you probably do. Attention spans are not what they were way back when; distraction/failure is just a click away. Remember that you can always work in steps. Break up your story if needed. Cut a lengthy press release and use supporting documentation such as technical fact sheets and testimonial pages instead. The chunking principle ("5 plus or minus two") is something I continue to utilize again and again. Create your own message release cycle, and reinforce your presence regularly. Bring a FAQ; if there is a question that needs to be asked and is not there, find the opportunity to bridge your message. Repetition breeds familiarity. Progressively reinforcing your call to action is goodness.

Don't touch it for 24 hours

Sometimes you need to walk away. From a project, from an argument, from work altogether. Give yourself a break and try to pace yourself; allow a day for things to settle down and for you to get a chance to breathe. Whilst that is usually not possible in a deadline-driven industry, it is something to aim for. The mad rush, non-stop emails, and continuous tweets often trigger reactions for emergencies that do not exist. Put the project down, clear your head, and come back with a fresh perspective. Step aside and regain your life.

Expect greatness

Keep your standards high and know your worth.

Part XIV.

Conferences and Sprints

34. People are Everything

Nóirín Plunkett

Nóirín Plunkett is a jack of all trades, and a master of several. A technical writer by day, her Open Source work epitomizes the saying "if you want something done, ask a busy person". Nóirín got her Open Source start at Apache, helping out with the httpd documentation project. Within a year, she had been recruited to the conference planning team, which she now leads. She was involved in setting up the Community Development project at Apache and has previously acted as Org Admin for the Google Summer of Code. She sits on the boards of both the Apache Software Foundation and the Open Cloud Initiative. When she's not online, Nóirín's natural habitat is the dance floor, although she's also a keen harpist and singer, and an excellent sous chef!

There is no such thing as a typical path, although mine was perhaps less typical than most. I first got a commit bit in my twenties, by which time I had already spent more than a year working at Microsoft. But after Microsoft I had moved to a foreign country to continue my studies, and it was nice to have a distraction, so I started working on various docs and translations, and I got a commit bit on the Apache httpd project.

As luck would have it, of course, ApacheCon EU was going to be held in Dublin the summer I was studying in Munich. But luck is kind to the Irish, and with only a little bit of wangling, I persuaded Sun Microsystems to sponsor me to attend the conference.

I have a photo of the moment I realized that this Open Source thing was for real, was going to change the world.

It was the evening before the conference. We still had not figured out where the fibre was terminated, that was supposed to make up our network backbone. We had checked every corner, cupboard and skirting, to no avail. We had given up for the night, and were busy trying to make sure that the rooms that would be hosting training classes the next day had at least enough connectivity for the trainers to demonstrate their material[1].

And as evening turned into night, and routers slowly revealed their Default Configuration secrets, half a dozen volunteers, people I had only met that afternoon, became friends.

I could not tell you where the half dozen girls I lived with that summer in Munich are now. But I am still in contact with each of the people you see in that picture. One of them has moved to a different country, another to a different continent. Most of them have changed jobs in the meantime, and I have graduated, taking up the grand Irish tradition of emigration to find employment.

You see, Open Source is all about the people. Really, on almost any project you would want to be a part of, the code comes second. People are what distinguish a project that is a joy to work on from one that is a chore; people are what make the difference between a project that is flourishing and one that languishes in the bitbucket. Sure, you will only stay up all night coding on a project if it is solving a problem you think is important; but unless you have people with whom you can collaborate, discuss, design, and develop, you are probably going to lose interest or get stuck before too long.

The true value of conferences, sprints, hackathons, retreats, or whatever your community calls their face-to-face moments, is exactly that. Coming face-to-face with the people you have been working with. Human beings are social animals; babies recognize faces even before they begin babbling, and no matter how good people are about being friendly and polite in email, there is something lost in those communications.

Meeting people face to face gives us an opportunity to recognize the humanity in those we might have struggled to get along with;

[1]The next morning, we checked up in the roof space, to try and find the fibre; still no joy. In the end, we found it in the comms cupboard of the nightclub in the basement next door.

to share the joy of a job well done with those we love to work with. Therefore, if I could have chosen one piece of advice, to hear when I was starting out, it would be to get out there, to meet people, to put faces to names at every opportunity[2].

And if you find the opportunities are few and far between, do not be afraid to ask. Look for people who are traveling near you, or who live where you are traveling; seek sponsorship to attend the larger community events; organize an event of your own!

It is the richness of our communities that makes Open Source what it is, and the shared striving towards common goals. And of course, the music sessions, the meals, the pints, and the parties! These are the things that bring us together, and you will find that once you have met people in person, even your email interactions will be much richer, much more fulfilling, and much more fruitful, than they had previously been.

[2]Sadly, I do say this with a caveat; as with any large gathering of people, there are risks to attending an Open Source conference. Some are worse than others, but in my own experience, assault in particular seems to be more prevalent in technical communities than in the non-technical. Seek out events that have a published code-of-conduct or anti-harassment policy, and ask for backup if you feel unsafe. The vast majority of the people you will find at an Open Source event are wonderful, caring human beings; I hope that in time, changing attitudes will stop the minority from thinking that they can get away with unreasonable behavior in these venues.

35. Getting People Together

Dave Neary

Dave Neary has been working on Free and Open Source projects since he discovered Linux in 1996. A long-time contributor to GNOME and the GIMP, he has worked full time helping companies come to terms with community-developed software since 2007. In that time, he has worked with projects including OpenWengo, Maemo and MeeGo on projects including event organization, community processes, product management and community metrics. As a volunteer, he has been involved in the organisation of GUADEC, the Desktop Summit, the Libre Graphics Meeting, the GIMP Conference, Ignite Lyon, the Open World Forum, and the MeeGo Conference.

One of the most important things you can do in a Free Software project, besides writing code, is to get your key contributors together as often as possible.

I have been fortunate to be able to organize a number of events in the past 10 years, and also to observe others and learn from them over that time. Here are some of the lessons I have learned over the years from that experience:

1. Venue

The starting point for most meetings or conferences is the venue. If you are getting a small group (under 10 people) together, then it is usually OK just to pick a city, and ask a friend who runs a business or is a college professor to book a room for you. Once you get bigger, you may need to go through a more formal process.

If you are not careful, the venue will be a huge expense, and you will have to find that money somewhere. But if you are smart, you can manage a free venue quite easily.

Here are a few strategies you might want to try:

- Piggy-back on another event – the Linux Foundation Collaboration Summit, OSCON, LinuxTag, GUADEC and many other conferences are happy to host workshops or meet-ups for smaller groups. The GIMP Developers Conference in 2004 was the first meet-up that I organized, and to avoid the hassle of dealing with a venue, finding a time that suited everyone, and so on, I asked the GNOME Foundation if they would not mind setting aside some space for us at GUADEC – and they said yes. Take advantage of the bigger conference's organization, and you get the added benefit of attending the bigger conference at the same time!

- Ask local universities for free rooms - This will not work once you go over a certain size, but especially for universities which have academics who are members of the local Linux User Group (LUG), they can talk their department head into booking a lecture theatre and a few classrooms for a weekend. Many universities will ask to do a press release and get credit on the conference website, and this is a completely fair deal. The first Libre Graphics Meeting was hosted free in CPE Lyon, and the GNOME Boston Summit has been hosted free for a number of years at MIT.

- If the venue can not be free, see if you can get someone else to pay for it. Once your conference is bigger than about 200 people, most venues will require payment. Hosting a conference will cost them a lot, and it is a big part of the business model of universities to host conferences when the students are gone. But just because the university or conference center will not host you for free that does not mean that you have to be the one paying. Local regional governments like to be involved with big events in their region. GUADEC in Stuttgart, the Gran Canaria Desktop Summit, and this year's Desktop Summit in Berlin have all had the cost of the venue covered by the host region. An additional benefit of partnering with the region is that they will often have links to local industry and press – resources you can use to get publicity and perhaps even sponsorship for your conference.

- Run a bidding process – by encouraging groups wishing to host the conference to put in bids, you are also encouraging them to source a venue and talk to local partners before you decide where to go. You are also putting cities in competition with each other, and like Olympic bids, cities do not like to lose competitions they are in!

2. Budget

Conferences cost money. Major costs for a small meet-up might be covering the travel costs of attendees. For a larger conference, the major costs will be equipment, staff and venue.

Every time I have been raising the budget for a conference, my rule of thumb has been simple:

1. Decide how much money you need to put on the event
2. Fundraise until you reach that amount
3. Stop fundraising, and move on to other things

Raising money is a tricky thing to do. You can literally spend all of your time doing it. At the end of the day, you have a conference to put on, and the amount of money in the budget is not the major concern of your attendees.

Remember, your primary goal is to get project participants together to advance the project. So getting the word out to prospective attendees, organizing accommodation, venue, talks, food and drinks, social activities and everything else people expect at an event is more important than raising money.

Of course, you need money to be able to do all the rest of that stuff, so finding sponsors, fixing sponsorship levels, and selling your conference is a necessary evil. But once you have reached the amount of money you need for the conference, you really do have better things to do with your time.

There are a few potential sources of funds to put on a conference – I recommend a mix of all of these as the best way to raise your budget.

- Attendees – While this is a controversial topic among many communities, I think it is completely valid to ask attendees to contribute something to the costs of the conference. Attendees benefit from the facilities, the social events, and gain value from the conference. Some communities consider attendance at their annual event as a kind of reward for services rendered, or an incentive to do good work in the coming year, but I do not think that's a healthy way to look at it. There are a few ways for conference attendees to fund the running of the conference:

    1. Registration fees – This is the most common way to get money from conference attendees. Most community conferences ask for a token amount of fees. I have seen conferences ask for an entrance fee of 20 to 50 Euro, and most people have not had a problem paying this. A pre-paid fee also has an additional benefit of massively reducing no-shows among locals. People place more value on attending an event that costs them 10 Euro than one where they can get in for free, even if the content is the same.

    2. Donations – This is very successfully employed by FOSDEM. Attendees are offered an array of goodies, provided by sponsors (books, magazine subscriptions, t-shirts) in return for a donation. But those who want can attend for free.

3. Selling merchandising – Perhaps your community would be happier hosting a free conference, and selling plush toys, t-shirts, hoodies, mugs and other merchandising to make some money. Beware: in my experience you can expect less from profits from merchandising sales than you would get giving a free t-shirt to each attendee with a registration fee.

- Sponsors – Media publications will typically agree to "press sponsorship" – providing free ads for your conference in their print magazine or website. If your conference is a registered non-profit which can accept tax-deductible donations, offer press sponsors the chance to invoice you for the services and then make a separate sponsorship grant to cover the bill. The end result for you is identical, but it will allow the publication to write off the space they donate to you for tax. What you really want, though, are cash sponsorships. As the number of Free Software projects and conferences has multiplied in recent years, the competition for sponsorship dollars has really heated up in recent years. To maximize your chances of making your budget target, there are a few things you can do.

  1. Conference brochure – Think of your conference as a product you are selling. What does it stand for, how much attention does it get, how important is it to you, to your members, to the industry and beyond? What is the value proposition for the sponsor? You can sell a sponsorship package on three or four different grounds: perhaps conference attendees are a high-value target audience for the sponsor, perhaps (especially for smaller conferences) the attendees are not what is important, it is the attention that the conference will get in the international press, or perhaps you are pitching to the company that the conference is improving a piece of software that they depend on. Depending on the positioning of the conference, you can then make a list of potential sponsors. You should have a

sponsorship brochure that you can send them, which will contain a description of the conference, a sales pitch explaining why it is interesting for the company to sponsor it, potentially press clippings or quotes from past attendees saying how great the conference is, and finally the amount of money you are looking for.

2. Sponsorship levels – These should be fixed based on the amount of money you want to raise. You should figure on your biggest sponsor providing somewhere between 30% and 40% of your total conference budget for a smaller conference. If you are lucky, and your conference gets a lot of sponsors, that might be as low as 20%. Figure on a third as a ball-park figure. That means if you have decided that you need 60,000 Euro then you should set your cornerstone sponsor level at 20,000 Euro, and all the other levels in consequence (say, 12,000 Euro for the second level and 6,000 Euro for third level). For smaller conferences and meet-ups, the fundraising process might be slightly more informal, but you should still think of the entire process as a sales pitch.

3. Calendar – Most companies have either a yearly or half-yearly budget cycle. If you get your submission to the right person at the right time, then you could potentially have a much easier conversation. The best time to submit proposals for sponsorship of a conference in the Summer is around October or November of the year before, when companies are finalizing their annual budget. If you miss this window, all is not lost, but any sponsorship you get will be coming out of discretionary budgets, which tend to get spread quite thin, and are guarded preciously by their owners. Alternatively, you might get a commitment to sponsor your July conference in May, at the end of the first half budget process - which is quite late in the day.

4. Approaching the right people – I am not going to teach anyone sales, but my personal secret to dealing with big organizations is to make friends with people inside the organizations, and try to get a feel for where the budget might come from for my event. Your friend will probably not be the person controlling the budget, but getting him or her on board is your opportunity to have an advocate inside the organization, working to put your proposal in front of the eyes of the person who owns the budget. Big organizations can be a hard nut to crack, but Free Software projects often have friends in high places. If you have seen the CTO or CEO of a Fortune 500 company talk about your project in a news article, do not hesitate to drop him or her a line mentioning that, and when the time comes to fund that conference, a personal note asking who the best person to talk to will work wonders. Remember, your goal is not to sell to your personal contact, it is to turn her into an advocate to your cause inside the organization, and create the opportunity to sell the conference to the budget owner later.

- Also, remember when you are selling sponsorship packages that everything which costs you money could potentially be part of a sponsorship package. Some companies will offer lanyards for attendees, or offer to pay for a coffee break, or ice cream in the afternoon, or a social event. These are potentially valuable sponsorship opportunities and you should be clear in your brochure about everything that is happening, and specify a provisional budget for each of these events when you are drafting your budget.

3. Content

Conference content is the most important thing about a conference. Different events handle content differently – some events invite a large proportion of their speakers, while others like GUADEC and OSCON invite proposals and choose talks to fill the spots.

The strategy you choose will depend largely on the nature of the event. If it is an event in its 10th year with an ever-increasing number of attendees, then a call for papers is great. If you are in your first year, and people really do not know what to make of the event, then setting the tone by inviting a number of speakers will do a great job of helping people know what you are aiming for.

For Ignite Lyon last year, I invited about 40% of the speakers for the first night (and often had to hassle them to put in a submission, and the remaining 60% came through a submission form. For the first Libre Graphics Meeting, apart from lightning talks, I think that I contacted every speaker first, except two people. Now that the event is in its 6th year, there is a call for proposals process which works quite well.

4. Schedule

It is hard to avoid putting talks in parallel which will appeal to the same people. Every single conference, you hear from people who wanted to attend talks which were on at the same time on similar topics.

My solution to conference scheduling is very low-tech, but works for me. Colored Post-it notes, with a different color for each theme, and an empty grid do the job fine. Write the talk titles one per Post-it, add any constraints you have for the speaker, and then fill in the grid.

Taking scheduling off the computer and into real objects makes it really easy to see when you have clashes, to swap talks as often as you like, and then to commit it to a web page when you are happy with it.

I used this technique successfully for GUADEC 2006[1] and Ross Burton re-used it successfully in 2007[2].

5. Parties

Parties are a trade-off. You want everyone to have fun, and hanging out is a huge part of attending a conference. But morning attendance suffers after a party. Pity the poor community member who has to drag himself out of bed after three hours sleep to go and talk to four people at 9am after the party.

Some conferences have too many parties. It is great to have the opportunity to get drunk with friends every night. But it is not great to *actually* get drunk with friends every night. Remember the goal of the conference: you want to encourage the advancement of your project.

I encourage one biggish party, and one other smallish party, over the course of the week. Outside of that, people will still get together, and have a good time, but it will be on their dime, and that will keep everyone reasonable.

With a little imagination, you can come up with events that do not involved loud music and alcohol. Other types of social events can work just as well, and be even more fun.

At GUADEC we have had a football tournament for the last number of years. During the OpenWengo Summit in 2007, we brought people on a boat ride on the Seine and we went on a classic 19th century merry-go-round afterwards. Getting people eating together is another great way to create closer ties. I have very fond memories of group dinners at a number of conferences. At the annual KDE conference Akademy, there is typically a Big Day Out, where people get together for a picnic, some light outdoors activity, a boat ride, some sightseeing or something similar.

[1] `http://blogs.gnome.org/bolsh/2006/05/09/initial-schedule-ready`
[2] `http://www.flickr.com/photos/rossburton/467140094`

6. Extra costs

Watch out for those unforeseen costs! One conference I was involved in, where the venue was "100% sponsored" left us with a 20,000 Euro bill for labor and equipment costs. Yes, the venue had been sponsored, but setting up tables and chairs, and equipment rental of whiteboards, overhead projectors and so on, had not. At the end of the day, I estimate that we used about 60% of the equipment we paid for.

Conference venues are hugely expensive for everything they provide. Coffee breaks can cost up to 10 US Dollars per person for a coffee and a few biscuits, bottled water for speakers costs 5 US Dollars per bottle, and so on. Rental of an overhead projector and microphones for one room for one day can cost 300 Euro or more, depending on whether the venue insists that equipment be operated by their A/V guy or not.

When you are dealing with a commercial venue, be clear up-front about what you are paying for.

7. On-site details

I like conferences that take care of the little details. As a speaker, I like it when someone contacts me before the conference and says they will be presenting me, what would I like them to say? It is reassuring to know that when I arrive there will be a hands-free mic and someone who can help fit it.

Taking care of all of these details needs a gaggle of volunteers, and it needs someone organizing them beforehand and during the event. Spend a lot of time talking to the local staff, especially the audio/visual engineers.

In one conference, the A/V guy would switch manually to a screensaver at the end of a presentation. We had a comical situation during a lightning talk session where after the first speaker, I switched presentations, and while the next presentation showed up on my laptop, we still had the screensaver on the big screen. No-one had talked to the A/V engineer to explain to him the format of the presentation! So we ended up with 4 Linux engineers looking at the laptop, checking connections and running various Xrandr incantations, trying to get the overhead projector working again! We eventually changed laptops, and the A/V engineer realized what the session was, and all went well after that – most of the people involved ended up blaming my laptop.

Running a conference, or even a smaller meet-up, is time-consuming, and consists of a lot of detail work, much of which will never be noticed by attendees. I have not even dealt with things like banners and posters, graphic design, dealing with the press, or any of the other joys that come from organizing a conference.

The end result is massively rewarding, though. A study I did last year of the GNOME project showed that there is a massive project-wide boost in productivity just after our annual conference, and many of our community members cite the conference as the high point of their year.

36. We're Not Crazy ... We're Conference Organizers!

Gareth J. Greenaway

Gareth J. Greenaway has been actively involved in the Free & Open Source community since 1997 after discovering Linux. A majority of this involvement has been gathering like-minded people to learn and experience new elements of Free & Open Source software. This involvement began with a small Linux Users Group and has expanded into organizing the Southern California Linux Expo, also known as SCALE. As one of the founding members of the event, Gareth current holds two key positions with the organization. The first role is Conference Operations and the second is Community Relations.

I started writing this section with what I saw as the requirements and steps for organizing a Free & Open Source conference, however, most of what I found myself saying had been covered by community management expert Dave Neary. So rather than repeat and overlap what Dave had to say, I decided to share various stories from organizing SCALE along with lessons that were learned over the years.

Too much power!

SCALE was started 9 years ago by members of three local Linux Users Group, growing out of a small regional event organized by one of these LUGs. The first time around was definitely a learning experience. Many lessons were learned, there was quite a bit of running around and the event seemed to fly by very quickly. Because none of us had planned an event where we had to be concerned about the load on electrical circuits or power usage, we had not considered it and because of that we ended up tripping the electrical breakers for the venue several times throughout the event.

It'll work ... its wireless!

The second SCALE included many of the lessons learned from the previous year but a new venue would result in new lessons. The Los Angeles Convention Center served as the location for SCALE 2, providing much more space to spread out for the event. The new location also served as our first lesson in contracts with a large organization for things such as A/V equipment, Internet access and exhibitor furniture.

Because of the placement for the event within the convention center, we were forced to locate the show's registration counters in an area that while visible to arriving attendees would be some distance away from the rest of the show. Our options for providing network access to the registration area were limited as fire regulations prevented running wire, so wireless was the only option. Everything was set up early the day for the show and was working great until mysteriously it was not. The wireless connection providing the much needed network access to the registration counter would simply disappear. There was much troubleshooting, much relocation of equipment and antennas and much frustration. "It should be working" was the only conclusion that everyone could come to, with little insight into why it simply was not working. Suddenly one of the team members, who had been standing some distance from the troubleshooting session, called everyone over to where he had been standing. In front of a large window which overlooked a large convention hall on the lower level, suddenly we all saw what it was he wanted us to see. Below us where dozens of flashing, spinning, pulsating lights staring up at us. Hundreds of electronic devices with flashing lights, sirens, blinking LED signs mockingly interfering with the wireless signals of our poor access points. We suddenly realized that our hours of working, attempting to solve this wireless issue had been futile. In the end we ran an Ethernet cable, taped it down securely as best we could and said a small prayer that the fire marshal would not make a surprise inspection.

Awards shows, snipers and the case of the missing IBM case

Perhaps one of the well-known stories from the history of SCALE is the mishaps and adventures that took place at SCALE 3. The adventures are well-known because as a SCALE attendee that year you could not help but experience them.

The third SCALE was set to take place once again at the L.A. Convention Center, the many months of planning and prep work had been done and everything was shaping up nicely. About 3 weeks prior to the event we received some information about various road closures around the convention center because of an upcoming awards show. The road closures resulted in there being one way in and out of the convention center, definitely not the ideal situation. Fortunately we had the time to alert everyone coming out for the show about the road closures and alternative routes. This was also the first year that SCALE would be a 2 day show, the hope being that things would be spread out a bit and not feel as rushed and hectic.

One of the long standing sponsors and exhibitors that SCALE has had over the years is IBM. They have always remained a welcome addition to the show, unfortunately their attendance is also usually met with some difficulty. The day before the event has typically been reserved as a setup day, an opportunity for the SCALE staff to set up and exhibitors to prepare their booths. It is also the day that any packages that exhibitors have delivered arrive. IBM had planned to showcase a new server line at the show and had had one of these servers shipped to the convention center, unfortunately it had not been delivered to their booth and no one at the convention center knew the whereabouts of the package. Many hours of searching all the possible locations within the convention center had not turned up any clues.

As it turned out, the awards show that would be taking place in a few days had rented a number of rooms for office space and storage needs. On a whim, the event coordinator who was assisting in the search suggested perhaps we search one of their storage rooms in hopes that the IBM case had been delivered there accidentally. The room in question was a small storage closet, inside we found boxes and boxes from the floor to the ceiling of tickets for the upcoming awards show. Behind these boxes, off in a corner was a large blue case with the IBM logo printed across it. Crisis averted!

The rest of the event ran smoothly and was relatively incident-free. As the event wound down a small crowd began to form near some large windows overlooking the street outside, as I walked past I realized what it was everyone was looking at. Several figures, all dressed in black, were moving around on the rooftops of the buildings across the street. All of these figures were carrying sniper rifles and were members of the Los Angeles Police Department's SWAT team, there in preparation for the awards show that would be starting a few hours from then. This definitely made for an exciting departure from the convention center.

No room at the inn

The fourth SCALE resulted in another venue change, this time the switch was to a hotel instead of a convention center. As the years went by, more and more people were traveling to attend SCALE and staying at local hotels, we decided to explore the possibility of holding SCALE in a hotel. We scouted the area and ended up working with an event coordinator on finding the right venue for the event. Settling on a hotel near the Los Angeles airport, the planning began. Holding an event at the hotel quickly became a source for new lessons on dealing with factors unique to a hotel. One of the most important lessons that we came to learn was making sure that all contracts had an agreed-upon cancellation policy.

Roughly five weeks prior to the event we received a call from the venue telling us that their corporate entity was canceling our event and giving our space to another event. Obviously this came as quite a shock and left us scrambling. The contract with the hotel did not include any sort of agreement for relocation, but simply stated that they could cancel the event without cause.

After many phone calls and negotiations with the original venue, eventually they were willing to provide some funds to help relocate to another venue. The new venue was also willing to honor the same terms regarding electrical, Internet access and A/V equipment. Everything worked out and the SCALE team had learned a valuable lesson when negotiating future contracts.

Curtain Call

All in all, organizing a conference is a rewarding endeavor and a great way to give back to the community. Conferences are an important element, they allow in person interaction in a world that commonly relies on virtual means of communication.

Advice I would give to future conference organizers would be:

- Start small, do not cram too much into an event the first year.
- Take chances, make mistakes, do not be afraid to fail.
- Communication is key!

37. How to Ask for Money

Selena Deckelmann

Selena Deckelmann is a major contributor to PostgreSQL. She speaks internationally about free software, developer communities and trolling. Her interests include opening up government data with the City of Portland, urban chickens and finding ways to make databases run faster.
She founded Postgres Open, a conference dedicated to the business of PostgreSQL and disruption of the database industry. She founded and co-chaired Open Source Bridge, a developer conference for open source citizens. She founded the PostgreSQL Conference, a successful series of east coast/west coast conferences in the US for PostgreSQL. She is currently on the program committees of PgCon and MySQL Users Conference, and OSCON data. She's a contributing writer for the Google Summer of Code Mentor Manual, and Student Guide. She is an advisor to the Ada Initiative and board member of Technocation, Inc.

Looking back since the first time I booted a PC into Linux in 1994, one thing stands out in my experience with open source: I wish I had known how to ask for money. Asking for money is hard. I have written grant proposals, asked for raises, negotiated salaries and consulting hourly rates, and raised funds for non-profit conferences. Through much trial and error, I have developed a process that works! What follows is a distillation of the tricks and techniques I have used over the last five years to raise money for unconferences, day-long code sprints and multi-day conferences about open source software and culture.

The process of getting money for a conference is really about six steps:

1. Identify a need.
2. Tell someone.
3. Ask for money.
4. Get the money.
5. Spend the money.
6. Say thank you.

Identify a need

Your first task as a conference organizer is to explain why you are putting on yet another conference, why that conference will be useful to attendees and why a sponsor should give you money to do it. This is called "writing a prospectus." The main elements of a prospectus are:

- Purpose: In a paragraph, explain why you are having the conference. What inspired you to bring people together? And who are the attendees? What will they talk about once they are there?

  If you have got a theme, or a specific goal in mind, mention that. Also, explain why you picked the location for the event. Is there some tie to the theme of the conference? Are the right people in that location? Was it sponsored by someone?

  Finally, share any interesting numbers from previous events, like number of attendees, interesting facts about speakers or details about your chosen location.

- Sponsorship opportunities and benefits: This section of the prospectus will outline what sponsors can expect from your conference. Typically, this is organized by dollar amount, but could also describe benefits for in-kind or volunteer work.

Start simple. Typically, sponsorships for events with cash are arranged by HR departments looking to hire, or marketing departments looking to advertise products or services.

The types of benefits sponsors ask for include: recognition on a website, mention of sponsorship in email or tweets out to attendees, access to email addresses and/or demographic information about attendees, logo and labels on conference tote-bags, lanyards or other swag, coffee breaks and lunch, parties, conference booth space and advertising space in a conference program.

Also, consider creative things that are unique to you, the conference and the location. For example, Portland has a very popular doughnut shop with a truck delivery service. We got a sponsor and then acquired permission to drive the truck right onto the grounds of our venue and served free doughnuts for breakfast.

Links to example prospectuses are below. They are all for big conferences, so YMMV. I have made a prospectus before that only had one option for sponsorship, and the benefits were: send one attendee from your company, and the organizers will publicly recognize your company and thank you for your sponsorship.

  - OSCON: `http://bit.ly/zd62Q6`
  - Open Source Bridge: `http://bit.ly/dKWvYJ`
  - MeeGo San Francisco: `http://bit.ly/zLUKEN`

- Contract: Always include a contract with your prospectus. This establishes basic expectations and timelines, and can save you a lot of trouble down the road.

  I am not a lawyer, and so what follows is my experience rather than legal advice. For smaller events, I write a very simple contract that outlines my expectations: sponsors promise to pay by a certain date, and I promise to hold the event on a certain date.

Copying an existing contract is a tricky business, as laws change and vary across states and countries. I consulted a lawyer that was recommended to me by an experienced open source community manager. The law firm was nice enough to create contracts and review contracts with hotels with us on a pro-bono basis. The Software Freedom Law Center may be able to refer you to an appropriate lawyer if you do not have one.

Now that you have created the prospectus, you need to talk to some people.

Tell someone

The most difficult step for me personally is getting the word out about my events!

Practice explaining your event in 1-2 sentences. Distill out what excites you, and what should excite other people.

Over the years, I have learned that I need to start talking RIGHT NOW to the people that I know, rather than worrying a whole lot about exactly the right people to tell. Make a list of people to talk to that you know already, and start checking them off.

The best way to start talking about what you are doing is in person or on the phone. This way, you are not spamming people, you have their attention, and you can get immediate feedback about your pitch. Do people get excited? Do they ask questions? Or do they get bored? Who else do they think you should talk to? Ask for feedback, and how you can make your pitch more appealing, interesting and worth their money!

Once you have your verbal pitch down, write it up and send a few emails. Ask for feedback on your email and always close the email with a call to action and a timeline for response. Keep track of who responds, how they respond and when you should follow up with each person.

Ask for money

Armed with your prospectus, and your finely tuned pitch, start approaching companies to fund your event. Whenever I start a new conference, I make a list of questions about my conference and answer each with a list of people and companies:

- Which people do I know who will think this is an amazing idea and will advocate for my event? (Cheerleaders)
- Who would be really fun to have around at the conference? (Mavens)
- Which companies have products that they want to pitch at my event? (Marketing)
- Who would want to hire the people who attend? (Recruiters)
- Which free and open source projects would like to recruit developers? (Open Source Recruiters)

Using these lists, send your prospectus out into the world! Here is an overview of how I organize the asking process: I start by sending prospectuses to my Cheerleaders. I also drop a copy of the prospectus with the Mavens, and invite them to attend the conference or speak. I then contact Marketing companies, Recruiters and Open Source Recruiters (sometimes there is overlap!). Meanwhile, I typically have opened registration for the conference and announced a few keynotes or special events. Hopefully this drives registrations a bit, and helps make sponsors feel like the conference is definitely going to happen, and that things are going well.

Get the money

If everything goes according to plan, companies and people start offering you money. When this happens you need two very important things:

- An invoice template
- A bank account to hold the money

Invoice templates are simple. I have a Google Spreadsheet that I just update for each invoice. You could easily use Open Office or even TeX (please, someone send me a LaTeX invoice template!) Examples of what invoices look like are available at `http://www.freetemplatesdepot.com`.

The most important elements of invoices are: the word INVOICE, a number for the invoice that is unique, the name and contact information of the sponsor, what the sponsor is expected to pay, terms of the invoice (when the sponsor should pay by, and what the penalty is for non-payment) and the total amount due. Then you need to send a copy of this form to the company. Keep a copy for yourself!

Some companies may require simple or complicated forms to be filled out and signed to identify you or your organization as a vendor. Paperwork. Ugh! Payment cycles for large companies can be up to two months. Also, budget cycles for companies are typically yearly. Find out whether a company even *has* available budget for your event, and whether you can get into their budget the following year if you missed the current year's window.

The bank account can be your personal bank account, but this puts you at risk. For a many-thousand-dollar event, you may wish to find an NGO or non-profit organization that can hold and dispense funds for you. If your conference is for-profit, you should consult an accountant about how to organize the funds. Finding a non-profit to work with may be as simple as contacting a foundation associated with an open source project.

Now on to what makes this whole process worthwhile - spending your hard-earned sponsorships!

Spend money

Now that your sponsors have paid, you can spend the money.

Create a budget that details what you want to spend money on, and when you will need to spend it. I recommend getting 3 quotes for products and services you are unfamiliar with, just so you can get a sense of what a fair price is. Let companies you are contacting know that you are going through a competitive bid process.

Once I establish a relationship with a company, I tend to do business with them year after year. I like having relationships with vendors, and find that even if I pay slightly more than if I aggressively bid things out every year, I end up saving time and getting better service from a vendor that knows me well.

For small events, you can keep track of expenses in a fairly simple spreadsheet. For larger projects, asking an accountant, or using dedicated accounting software can help. Here is a list of Quicken alternatives that are free (to varying degrees and in varying aspects!): `http://bit.ly/9RRgu0`

What is most important is to keep track of all your expenses, and to not spend money that you do not have! If you are working with a non-profit to manage the event's money, ask them for help and advice before getting started.

Say thank you

There are many ways to say thank you to the people and companies that supported your event. Most importantly, follow up on all the promises you made in the prospectus. Communicate as each commitment is met!

During the event, find ways of connecting with the sponsors, by designating a volunteer to check in with them and checking in with them yourself.

After the event, be sure to individually thank sponsors and volunteers for their contributions. A non-profit I work with sends thank-you notes individually to each sponsor at the start of the new year.

Generally speaking, communication is the compost of fundraising! Giving attention and building genuine relationships with sponsors helps find more sponsors, and build your reputation as a great event organizer.

Lessons learned

After creating and running dozens of events, the two most important aspects of it all have been finding mentors and learning to communicate well.

Mentors helped me turn rants into essays, messes into prospectuses, and difficult conversations into opportunities. I found mentors at companies that sponsored my conferences and gave detailed, sometimes painful, feedback. And I found mentors among volunteers who dedicated hundreds of hours to write software for my events, recruit speakers, document what we were doing, and carry the conference on after me.

Learning to communicate well takes time, and the opportunity to make a lot of mistakes. I learned the hard way that not developing a relationship with the best sponsors means no sponsorship the following year! I also found that people are incredibly forgiving when mistakes happen, as long as you communicate early and often.

Good luck with your fundraising, and please let me know if you find this helpful.

Part XV.

Business

38. Free Software in Public Administrations

Till Adam

Originally from a liberal arts and music background, Till Adam has spent the last decade or so in software. He works at KDAB where he directs services, including the company's Free Software activities. Till also serves on the board of directors of Kolab Systems AG, a company with a pure Free Software business model. He lives with his wife and daughter in Berlin.

Introduction

Like, I imagine, many of the other authors in this collection of essays I started contributing to Free Software when I was a student. I had decided relatively late in life to pursue a degree in Computer Science (having failed to become rich and famous as a musician) and was expecting to be quite a bit older than my peers when I graduated. So I thought it would be good to teach myself programming, which I was not getting much of at school, to become more attractive to future employers, despite my age. After some forays into various smaller communities I eventually found my way into KDE and started working on the email application. Thanks to the extremely helpful and technically brilliant group of people I met there I was able to learn quickly and contribute meaningfully to the code base, getting sucked more and more into both the social circle and the fascinating technical problem space of personal information management.

When KDAB, a company full of KDE people, asked me whether I wanted to help out with some commercial work that was being done, as a student job, I was of course thrilled to be able to combine making a living with my hobby of hacking on KDE software. Over the years I then witnessed the adoption of KDE's personal information management frameworks and applications by the public sector, particularly in Germany, first hand and saw KDAB's business in this area grow. As I transitioned into more coordinative roles it eventually became part of my job to effectively sell and deliver services based on Free Software including KDE's products to large organizations, particularly in the public sector.

It should be noted that much of the project work this text reflects upon was done in cooperation with other Free Software businesses, namely g10code, the maintainers of GNUPG and cryptography specialists, and Intevation, a consultancy focused entirely on Free Software and its strategic challenges and opportunities. Especially Bernhard Reiter, one of Intevation's founders, was instrumental to the selling and running of many of these projects and whatever morsels of wisdom this text might contain are likely products of his analysis and my many conversations with him over the years.

So if Bernhard and I could travel back in time and share insights with our younger, more naïve selves, what would those insights be? Well, it turns out they all start with the letter 'P'.

People

As things stand today it is still harder for IT operations people and decision makers to use Free Software than it is to use proprietary alternatives. Even in Germany, where Free Software has relatively strong political backing, it is easier and safer to suggest the use of something that is perceived as "industry standard" or "what everyone else does"; proprietary solutions, in other words. Someone who proposes a Free Software solution will likely face opposition by less adventurous (or more short-sighted) colleagues, close scrutiny by superiors, higher expectations with respect to the results and unrealistic budget pressure. It thus requires a special breed of person willing to take personal risks, go out on a limb, potentially jeopardize career progress and fight an uphill battle. This is of course true in any organization, but in a public administration special persistence is required because things move generally more slowly and an inflexible organizational hierarchy and limited career options amplify the issue.

Without an ally on the inside it can be prohibitively difficult to get Free Software options seriously considered. If there is such a person, it is important to support them in their internal struggles as much as possible. This means providing them with timely, reliable and verifiable information about what goes on in the community the organization intends to interface with, including enough detail to provide a full picture but reducing the complexity of the communication and planing chaos that is part of the Free Software way of working, at times, such that it becomes more manageable and less threatening. Honesty and reliability help to build strong relationships with these key people, the basis of longer term success. As their interface to the wondrous and somewhat frightening world of Free Software communities they rely on you to find the paths that will carry them and their organization to their goals and they make decisions largely based on personal trusts. That trust has to be earned and maintained.

In order to achieve this, it is important to focus not only on achieving the technical results of projects, but also keep in mind the broader personal and organizational goals of those one is dealing with. Success or failure of the current project might not depend on whether an agency's project manager can show off only marginally related functionality to superiors at seemingly random points in the schedule, but whether the next project happens or not might. When you have few friends, helping them be successful is a good investment.

Priorities

As technologists, Free Software people tend to focus on the things that are new, exciting and seemingly important at a technology level. Consequently we put less emphasis on things that are more important in the context of an (often large) public administration. But consider someone wanting to roll out a set of technologies in an organization that intends to stick with it for a long time. Since disruptive change it difficult and expensive, it is far more important to have documentation of the things that will not work, so they can be avoided or worked around, than it is to know that some future version will behave much better. It is unlikely that that new version will ever be practically available to the users currently under consideration, and it is far easier to deal with known issues pro-actively than to be forced to react to surprises. Today's documented bug is, ironically, often preferable to tomorrow's fix with unforeseeable side effects.

In a large organization that uses software for a long time, the cost of acquiring the software, be it via licenses or as part of contracted custom development of Free Software, pales in comparison to the cost of maintaining and supporting it. This leads to the thinking that fewer, more stable features, which cause less load on the support organization and are more reliable and less maintenance intensive are better than new, complex and likely less mature bells and whistles.

While both of these sentiments run counter to the instincts of Free Software developers, it is these same aspects that make it very attractive for the public sector to contract the development of Free Software, rather than spending the money on licenses for off-the-shelf products. Starting from a large pool of freely available software, the organization can invest the budgets it has into maturing exactly those parts that are relevant for its own operations. It thus does not have to pay (via license costs) for the development of market driven, fancy features it will not need. By submitting all of that work back upstream into the community, the longer term maintenance of these improvements and of the base software is shared amongst many. Additionally, because all of the improvements become publicly available, other organizations with similar needs can benefit from them with no additional cost, thus maximizing the impact of tax payer money, something any public administration is (or should be) keen to do.

Procurement

So, if it is so clearly better use of IT budgets for government agencies to invest into the improvement of Free Software and into the tailoring of it to its needs, why is it so rarely done? Feature parity for many of the most important kinds of software has long been reached, usability is comparable, robustness and total cost of ownership as well. Mindshare and knowledge are of course still problems, but the key practical obstacle for procurement of Free Software services lies in the legal and administrative conditions under which it must happen. Changing these conditions requires work on a political and lobby level. In the context of an individual project it is rarely possible. Thankfully organizations like the Free Software Foundation Europe and its sister organization in the US are lobbying on our behalf and slowly effecting change. Let's look at two central, structural problems.

Licenses, not Services Many IT budgets are structured such that part of the money is set aside for the purchase of new software or the continued payment for the use of software in the form of licenses. Since it was unimaginable to those who structured these budgets that software could ever be anything but a purchasable good, represented by a proprietary license, it is often difficult or impossible for the IT decision makers to spend that same money on services. Managerial accounting will simply not hear of it. This can lead to the unhappy situation that an organization has the will and the money to improve a piece of Free Software to exactly suit its needs, deploy and run it for years and contribute the changes back to community, yet the plan can not go forward unless the whole affair is wrapped in an artificial and unnecessary sale and purchase of an imaginary product based on the Free Software license.

Legal Traps Contractual frameworks for software providers often assume that whoever signs up to provide the software fully controls all of the involved copyrights, trademarks and patents. The buying organization expects to be indemnified against various risks by the provider. In the case of a company or an individual providing a solution or service based on Free Software that is often impossible since there are other rights holders that can not reasonably be involved in the contractual arrangement. This problem appears most pointedly in the context of software patents. It is practically impossible for a service provider to insure against patent litigation risks which makes it very risky to take on the full responsibility.

Price

Historically, the key selling point of Free Software that has been communicated to the wider public has been its potential to save money. Free Software has indeed made large scale cost saving possible in many organizations and for many years now. The GNU/Linux operating system has spearheaded this development. Because of its free availability for download was perceived in stark contrast to the expensive licenses of its main competitor, Microsoft Windows. For something as widely used and useful as an operating system, the structural cost benefit of development cost put onto many shoulders is undeniable. Unfortunately the expectation that this holds true for all Free Software products has led to the unrealistic view that using it will always, immediately and greatly reduce cost. In our experience, this is not true. As we have seen in earlier sections it does make a lot of sense to get more out of the money spent using Free Software and it is likely that over time and across multiple organizations money can be saved, but for the individual agency looking to deploy a piece of Free Software there will be an upfront investment and cost associated with getting it to the point of maturity and robustness required.

While this seems entirely reasonable to IT operations professionals it is often harder to convince their superiors with budget power of this truth. Especially when potential cost saving has been used as an argument to get Free Software in the door initially it can prove very challenging to effectively manage expectations down the road. The earlier the true cost and nature of the investment is made transparent to decision makers, the more likely they are to commit to it for the long haul. High value for money is still attractive and a software services provider that will not continue to be available because the high price pressure does not yield sufficient economic success is as unattractive in Free Software as it is in proprietary license based business models. It is thus also in the interest of the customers that cost estimations are realistic and the economic conditions of the work being done are sustainable.

Conclusion

Our experience shows that it is possible to convince organizations in the public sector to spend money on Free Software based services. It is an attractive proposition that provides good value and makes political sense. Unfortunately structural barriers still exist, but with the help of pioneers in the public sector they can be worked around. Given sufficient support by us all, those working for Free Software on a political level will eventually overcome them. Honest and clear communication of the technical and economic realities can foster effective partnerships that yield benefits for the Free Software community, the public administrations using the software and those providing them with the necessary services in an economically viable, sustainable way.

39. Underestimating the Value of a Free Software Business Model

Frank Karlitschek

Frank Karlitschek was born in 1973 in Reutlingen, Germany and started to write software at the age of 11. He studied Computer Science at the University of Tübingen and became involved in free software and Internet technologies in the mid-1990s. In 2001, he started to contribute to KDE by launching KDE-Look.org, an artwork community site which later became the openDesktop.org network. Frank started several Open Source projects and initiatives like the Social Desktop, the Open Collaboration Services, the Open-PC and ownCloud. In 2007 he started a company called hive01 which offers services and products around Open Source and Internet technologies. Today Frank is a board member and Vice President of the KDE e.V. and a regular speaker at international conferences.

Introduction

Ten years ago, I underestimated the value of a business model. Free software and a business model? They do not belong together. At least, that is what I thought when I started contributing to KDE in 2001. Free Software is about fun and not money. Right? Free software people want a world where everybody can write software and huge companies, like Microsoft or Google, are superfluous. Software should be free and anyone who wants to develop software should be able to do so – even hobby developers. So earning money is not important. Right? Today, I hold a different opinion. Sometimes developers should be remunerated for their efforts.

The Free Software motivation

Most Free Software developers have two basic motivations to work on Free Software. The first motivation is the fun factor. It is a fantastic experience to work together with very talented people from all over the world and create great technology. KDE, for example, is one of the most welcoming communities I know. It is so much fun to work with thousands of contributors from all over the world to create software which will be used by millions. Basically, everyone is an expert in one or more areas and we collaborate to create a shared vision. For me it is always a blast to meet other KDE contributors, exchange ideas or work on our software whether we meet online or in real life at one of the many conferences or events. And it is also about friendship. Over the years I have made many good friends in KDE.

But KDE contributors are not motivated only by fun to join KDE. It is also the idea that all of us can make the world a better place with our contributions. Free Software is essential if you care about access to technology and IT for developing countries. It enables poor people to participate in the information age without buying expensive licenses for proprietary software. It is essential for people who care about privacy and security, because Free Software is the only way to see exactly what your computer is doing with your private data. Free Software is important for a healthy IT eco-system, because it enables everybody to build on the work of others and really innovate. Without Free Software it would not have been possible for Google or Facebook to start their businesses. It is not possible to innovate and create the next disruptive technology if you depend on proprietary software and do not have full access to all parts of the software.

Free Software is also essential for education, because everybody can see all the internals of the software and study how it works. That is how Free Software helps to make the world a better place and why I contribute to Free Software projects such as KDE.

The need for an ecosystem

These are the main reasons why I want to see Free Software, and especially the free desktop, become mainstream. To make this happen, we need a lot more contributors than we have today. By contributors I mean people who write the core frameworks, the desktop, the great applications. We need people who work on usability, artwork, promotion and many other important areas. KDE is already a really big community with thousands of members. But we need more people to help to compete with proprietary software in a big way. The Free Software community is tiny compared to the proprietary software world. On the one hand this is not a problem, because the distributed software development model of the Free Software world is much more efficient than the closed source way of writing software. One big advantage is, for example, the ability to re-use code better. But even with these advantages we need many more contributors than we have today, if we really want to conquer the desktop and mobile markets.

We also need companies to help us bring our work to the mass market. In a nutshell, we need a big and healthy ecosystem that enables people to work on Free Software for a living.

The current situation

I started contributing to KDE over 10 years ago and since then I have seen countless highly motivated and talented people join KDE. This is really cool. The problem is that I also saw a lot of experienced contributors dropping out of KDE. That is really sad. Sometimes it is just the normal way of the world. Priorities shift and people concentrate on other stuff. The problem is that many also drop out because of money. At some point people graduate and want to move out of their dorm rooms. Later some people want to get married and have kids. At this point people have to find jobs. There are some companies in the KDE ecosystem that offer KDE-related jobs. But these are only a fraction of the available IT jobs. So, a lot of senior KDE contributors have to work for companies where they work on proprietary software, unrelated to KDE and Free Software. Sooner or later most of these developers drop out of KDE. I underestimated this factor 10 years ago, but I think it is a problem for KDE in the long term, because we lose our most experienced people to proprietary software companies.

My dream world

In my dream world people can pay their rent by working on Free Software and they can do it in a way which does not conflict with our values. KDE contributors should have all the time they need to contribute to KDE and Free Software in general. They should earn money by helping KDE. Their hobbies should become their jobs. This would make KDE grow in a big way, because it would be fun to contribute and also provide good long-term job prospects.

What are the options?

So what are the options? What can we do to make this happen? Are there ways for developers to pay their rent while working on Free Software? I want to list a few ideas here that I collected during several discussions with Free Software contributors. Some of them are probably controversial, because they introduce completely new ideas into the Free Software world. But I think it is essential for us to think beyond our current world if we want to be successful with our mission.

Sponsored development Today, more and more companies appreciate the importance of Free Software and contribute to Free Software projects, or even release their own completely Free Software projects. This is an opportunity for Free Software developers. We should talk to more companies and convince them to work with the Free Software world.

End-user donations There should be an easy way for end-users to donate money directly to developers. If a user of a popular application wants to support the developer and promote the further development of the application, donating money should be just one mouse click away. The donation system can be built into the application to make it as easy as possible to send money.

Bounties The idea behind bounties is that one or more users of an application can pay for the development of a specific feature. A user can list his feature request on a website and say how much he is willing to pay for the feature. Other users who also like the same feature may add some money to the feature request. At some point the developer starts to develop the feature and collects the money from the users. This bounty feature is not easy to implement. People already tried to set up a system like this and failed. But I think it can work if we do it right.

Support The idea is that the developer of an application sells direct support to the users of the application. For example, the users of an application buy support for, let us say, $5 a month and get the right to call the developer directly at specified times of the day, users may post questions to a specific email address, or the developer can even help the users via a remote desktop. I realize many developers will not like the idea that users call them and ask strange questions, but if this means that they earn enough with the support system to work full-time on their applications, then it must be a good thing.

Supporters This is the idea that end-users can become supporters of an application. The "Become a Supporter" button would be directly built into the application. The user then becomes a supporter for a monthly payment of, for example $5, which goes directly to the developer. All the supporters are listed in the About Dialog of the application together with their photos and real names. Once a year all supporters are also invited to a special supporter party together with the developers. It is possible that a developer may be able to work full-time on an application, if enough users become supporters.

Affiliate programs Some applications have integrated web services and some of these web services run affiliate programs. For example, a media player can be integrated in the Amazon mp3 MusicStore or a PDF reader can be integrated in an ebook store. Every time a user buys content via the application, the developer gets some money.

App store for application binaries Many people do not know that it is possible to sell binaries of Free Software. The GPL only requires that you also provide the source code. So, it is perfectly legal and OK to sell nicely packaged binaries of our software. In fact, companies such as Redhat and Novell already sell our software in their commercial distributions but the developers do not benefit from it directly. All the revenue goes to the companies and nothing to the developers. So we could enable the Free Software developers to sell nicely packaged, optimized and tested applications to the end-user. This might work especially well on Mac or Windows. I am sure a lot of users would pay $3 for an Amarok Windows binary, or digiKam for Mac, if all the money went directly to the developer.

Conclusion

Most of these ideas are not easy to implement. They require changes to our software, changes to our ways of working and changes among our users who must be encouraged to show they value the software we create by helping to fund its development.

However, the potential benefits are huge. If we can secure revenue streams for our software we can retain our best contributors and maybe attract new ones. Our users will get a better experience with faster software development, the ability to directly influence development through bounties and better support.

Free Software is no longer just a hobby to be done in your spare time. It is time to make it a business.

40. Free and Open Source-Based Business Models

Carlo Daffara

Carlo Daffara is a researcher in the field of Open Source-based business models, collaborative development of digital artifacts, and Open Source software employment in companies. He is part of the editorial review board of the International Journal of Open Source Software & Processes (IJOSSP) and member of the technical board of two regional Open Source competence centers, as well as member of the FSFE European Legal Network. He has been part of SC34 and JTC1 committees in the Italian branch of ISO, UNINFO; and participated in the Internet Society Public Software working group, and many other standardization-related initiatives. Previous to that, Carlo Daffara was the Italian representative at the European Working Group on Libre Software, the first EU initiative in support of Open Source and Free Software. He chaired the SME working group of the EU Task Force on Competitiveness, and the IEEE open source middleware working group of the Technical Committee on Scalable Computing. He worked as project reviewer for the EC in the field of international collaboration, software engineering, open source and distributed systems and was Principal Investigator in several EU research projects.

Introduction

"How do you make money with Free Software?" was a very common question just a few years ago. Today, that question has evolved into

"What are successful business strategies that can be implemented on top of FLOSS?" The question is not as gratuitous as it may seem, as many academic researchers still write this kind of text: "Open-source software is deliberately developed outside of market mechanisms ... fails to contribute to the creation of value in development, as opposed to the commercial software market ... does not generate profit, income, jobs or taxes ... The open-source licenses on the software aim to suppress any ownership claims to the software and prevent prices from being established for it. In the end, the developed software cannot be used to generate profit." [Koot 03] or [Eng 10] claims that "economists showed that real world open source collaborations rely on many different incentives such as education, signaling, and reputation." (without any mention of economic incentives). This purely "social" view of FLOSS is biased and wrong, and we will demonstrate that there are economical reasons behind the success of Free/Open Source businesses that go beyond the purely pro-bono collaborations.

FLOSS and Economic Realities

In most areas, the use of FLOSS brings a substantial economic advantage, thanks to the shared development and maintenance costs, already described by researchers like Gosh, that estimated an average R&D cost reduction of 36%. The large share of "internal" FLOSS deployments explains why some of the economic benefits are not perceived directly in the business service market.

The FLOSSIMPACT study found in 2006 that companies contributing code to FLOSS projects have in total at least 570 thousand employees and an annual revenue of 263B Euro [Gosh 06], thus making Open Source and Free Software among the most important ICT-based economic phenomenons. It is also important to recognize that a substantial percentage of this economic value is not immediately visible in the marketplace, as the majority of software is not developed with the intent of selling it (the so-called "shrinkwrap" software) but is developed for internal use only. As identified by the FISTERA EU thematic network in fact the majority of software is developed for internal use only:

Region	Proprietary software licenses	Software services (development/customization)	Internal development
EU-15	19%	52%	29%
US	16%	41%	43%
Japan	N/A	N/A	32%

It is clear that what we call "the software market" is in reality much smaller than the real market for software and services, and that 80% of it is invisible. We will see that FLOSS has a major part of the economic market directly through this "internal" development model.

Business Models and Value Proposition

The basic idea behind business models is quite simple: I have something or can do something – the "value proposition" – and it is more economical to pay me to do or get this "something" instead of doing it yourself (sometimes it may even be impossible to find alternatives, as in natural or man-made monopolies, so the idea of doing it myself may not be applicable). There are two possible sources for the value: a property (something that can be transferred) and efficiency (something that is inherent in what the company does, and how they do it). With Open Source, usually "property" is non-exclusive (with the exception of what is called "Open Core", where some part of the code is not open at all, and that will be covered later in the article). Other examples of property are trademarks, patents, licenses ... anything that may be transferred to another entity through a contract or legal transaction. Efficiency is the ability to perform an action with a lower cost (both tangible and intangible), and is something that follows the specialization in a work area or appears thanks to a new technology. Examples of the first are simply the decrease in time necessary to perform an action when you increase your expertise in it; the first time you install a complex system it may require a lot of effort, and this effort is reduced the more experience you have with the tasks necessary to perform the installation itself; examples of the second may be the introduction of a tool that simplifies the process (for example, through image cloning) and it introduces a huge discontinuity, a "jump" in the graph of efficiency versus time.

These two aspects are the basis of all the business models that we have analyzed in the past; it is possible to show that all of them fall in a continuum between properties and efficiency.

Among the results of our past research project, one thing that we found is that property-based projects tend to have lower contributions from the outside, because it requires a legal transaction to become part of the company's properties; think for example about dual licensing: for his code to become part of the product source code, an external contributor needs to sign off his rights to the code, to allow the company to sell the enterprise version alongside the open one.

On the other hand, right-handed models based purely on efficiency tends to have higher contributions and visibility, but lower monetization rates. As I wrote many times, there is no ideal business model, but a spectrum of possible models, and companies should adapt themselves to changing market conditions and adapt their model as well. Some companies start as pure efficiency based, and build an internal property with time; some others may start as property based, and move to the other side to increase contributions and reduce the engineering effort (or enlarge the user base, to create alternative ways of monetizing users).

A Business Models Taxonomy

The EU FLOSSMETRICS study on Free Software-based business models created, after an analysis of more than 200 companies, a taxonomy of the main business models used by Open Source companies; the main models identified in the market are:

- Dual licensing: the same software code distributed under the GPL and a proprietary license. This model is mainly used by producers of developer-oriented tools and software, and works thanks to the strong coupling clause of the GPL, that requires derivative works or software directly linked to be covered under the same license. Companies not willing to release their own software under the GPL can obtain a proprietary license that provides an exemption from the distribution conditions of the GPL, which seems desirable to some parties. The downside of dual licensing is that external contributors must accept the same licensing regime, and this has been shown to reduce the volume of external contributions, which are limited mainly to bug fixes and small additions.

- Open Core (previously called "proprietary value-add" or "split Free Software/proprietary"): this model distinguishes between a basic Free Software and a proprietary version, based on the Free Software one but with the addition of proprietary plug-ins. Most companies following such a model adopt the Mozilla Public License, as it allows explicitly this form of intermixing, and allows for much greater participation from external contributions without the same requirements for copyright consolidation as in dual licensing. The model has the intrinsic downside that the Free Software product must be valuable to be attractive for the users, i.e. it should not be reduced to "crippleware", yet at the same time should not cannibalize the proprietary product. This balance is difficult to achieve and maintain over time; also, if the software is of large interest, developers may try to complete the missing functionality in

Free Software, thus reducing the attractiveness of the proprietary version and potentially giving rise to a full Free Software competitor that will not be limited in the same way.

- Product specialists: companies that created or maintain a specific software project and use a Free Software license to distribute it. The main revenues are provided from services like training and consulting and follow the original "best code here" and "best knowledge here" of the original EUWG classification [DB 00]. It leverages the assumption, commonly held, that the most knowledgeable experts on a software are those who have developed it, and this way can provide services with a limited marketing effort, by leveraging the free redistribution of the code. The downside of the model is that there is a limited barrier of entry for potential competitors, as the only investment that is needed is in the acquisition of specific skills and expertise on the software itself.

- Platform providers: companies that provide selection, support, integration and services on a set of projects, collectively forming a tested and verified platform. In this sense, even GNU/Linux distributions were classified as platforms; the interesting observation is that those distributions are licensed for a significant part under Free Software licenses to maximize external contributions, and leverage copyright protection to prevent outright copying but not "cloning" (the removal of copyrighted material like logos and trademark to create a new product)[1]. The main value proposition comes in the form of guaranteed quality, stability and reliability, and the certainty of support for business critical applications.

- Selection/consulting companies: companies in this class are not strictly developers, but provide consulting and selection/ evaluation services on a wide range of projects, in a way that

[1] Examples of RedHat clones are CentOS and Oracle Linux.

is close to the analyst role. These companies tend to have very limited impact on the communities, as the evaluation results and the evaluation process are usually a proprietary asset.

- Aggregate support providers: companies that provide a one-stop support on several separate Free Software products, usually by directly employing developers or forwarding support requests to second-stage product specialists.
- Legal certification and consulting: these companies do not provide any specific code activity, but provide support in checking license compliance, sometimes also providing coverage and insurance for legal attacks; some companies employ tools for verify that code is not improperly reused across company boundaries or in an improper way.
- Training and documentation: companies that offer courses, online and physical training, additional documentation or manuals. This is usually offered as part of a support contract, but recently several large scale training center networks started offering Free Software-specific courses.
- R&D cost sharing: A company or organization may need a new or improved version of a software package, and fund some consultant or software manufacturer to do the work. Later on, the resulting software is redistributed as Open Source to take advantage of the large pool of skilled developers who can debug and improve it. A good example is the Maemo platform, used by Nokia on its Mobile Internet Devices (like the N810); within Maemo, only 7.5% of the code is proprietary, with a reduction in costs estimated around 228M$ (and a reduction in time-to-market of one year). Another example is the Eclipse ecosystem, an integrated development environment (IDE) originally released as Free Software by IBM and later managed by the Eclipse Foundation. Many companies adopted Eclipse as a basis for their own product, and this way reduced the overall cost of creating a software product that provides in some

way developer-oriented functionality. There is a large number of companies, universities and individual that participate in the Eclipse ecosystem. As recently measured, IBM contributes around 46% of the project, with individuals accounting for 25%, and a large number of companies like Oracle, Borland, Actuate and many others with percentages that go from 1 to 7%. This is similar to the results obtained from analysis of the Linux kernel, and show that when there is a healthy and large ecosystem the shared work reduces engineering cost significantly; in [Gosh 06] it is estimated that it is possible to obtain savings in terms of software research and development of 36% through the use of Free Software; this is, in itself, the largest actual "market" for Free Software, as demonstrated by the fact that the majority of developers are using at least some Free Software within their own code (56.2%, as reported in [ED 05]). Another excellent example of "coopetition" among companies is the WebKit project, the HTML rendering engine that is at the basis of the Google Chrome browser, Apple Safari and is used in the majority of mobile devices. In the project, after an initial 1 year delay, the number of outside contributions start to become significant, and after a little more than 1 and a half year they surpass those performed by Apple by a substantial margin - thus reducing the maintenance costs and the engineering effort, thanks to the division of work among co-developers.

- Indirect revenues: A company may decide to fund Free Software projects if those projects can create a significant revenue source for related products, not directly connected with source code or software. One of the most common cases is the writing of software needed to run hardware, for instance, operating system drivers for specific hardware. In fact, many hardware manufacturers are already distributing gratis software drivers. Some of them are already distributing some of their drivers (specially those for the Linux kernel) as Free Software. The loss-leader is a traditional commercial model, common also outside of the world of software; in this model, effort is invested in a FLOSS project to create or extend another market under different conditions. For example, hardware vendors invest in the development of software drivers for Free Software operating systems (like GNU/Linux) to extend the market of the hardware itself. Other ancillary models are for example those of the Mozilla foundation, which obtains a non-trivial amount of money from a search engine partnership with Google (an estimated 72M$ in 2006), while SourceForge/OSTG receives the majority of revenues from e-commerce sales of the affiliate ThinkGeek site.

Some companies have more than one principal model, and thus are counted twice; in particular, most dual licensing companies are also selling support services, and thus are marked as both. Also, product specialists are counted only when there is a demonstrable participation of the company in the project as "main committer"; otherwise, the number of specialists would be much greater, as some projects are the center of commercial support for many companies (good examples include OpenBravo or Zope).

Another relevant consideration is the fact that platform providers, while limited in number, tend to have a much larger revenue rate than both specialists or open core companies. Many researchers are trying to identify whether there is a more "efficient" model among all those surveyed; what we found is that the most probable future outcome will be a continuous shift across models, with a long-term consolidation of development consortia (like the Eclipse or Apache consortium) that provide strong legal infrastructure and development advantages, and product specialists that provide vertical offerings for specific markets.

Conclusions

FLOSS not only allows for sustainable, and even very large market presence (RedHat is already quite close to 1B$ in annual revenues) but also many different models that are totally impossible with proprietary software. The fact that FLOSS is a non-rival good also facilitates cooperation between companies, both to increase the geographic base and to be able to engage large scale contracts that may require multiple competencies, both geographical (same product or service, different geographical areas); "vertical" (among products) or "horizontal" (among activities). This facilitation of new ecosystems is one of the reasons why FLOSS is now present in nearly all the IT infrastructures in the world, increasing value and helping companies and Public Administrations in reducing costs and collaborating together for better software.

References

- [*DB*00] Daffara, C. Barahona, J.B. Free Software/Open Source: Information Society Opportunities for Europe? working paper, `http://eu.conecta.it` paper, OSSEMP workshop, Third international conference on open source. Limerick 2007

- [*ED*05] Evans Data, Open Source Vision report, 2005

- [*Eng*10] Engelhardt S. Maurer S. The New (Commercial) Open Source: Does it Really Improve Social Welfare? Goldman School of Public Policy Working Paper No. GSPP10-001, 2010

- [*Gar*06] Gartner Group, Open source going mainstream. Gartner report, 2006

- [*Gosh*06] Gosh, et al. Economic impact of FLOSS on innovation and competitiveness of the EU ICT sector. `http://bit.ly/cNwUz0`

- [*Koot*03] Kooths, S. Langenfurth, M. Kalwey, N. Open-Source Software: An Economic Assessment Technical report, Muenster Institute for Computational Economics (MICE), University of Muenster

Part XVI.

Legal and Policy

41. On being a Lawyer in FOSS

Till Jaeger

Dr. Till Jaeger has been a partner at JBB Rechtsanwaelte since 2001. He is a Certified Copyright and Media Law Attorney and advises large and medium-sized IT businesses as well as government authorities and software developers on matters involving contracts, licensing and online use. One particular focus of his work is on the legal issues created by Free and Open Source Software. He is co-founder of the Institute for Legal Aspects of Free & Open Source Software (ifrOSS). He provides advice on compliance with open source licenses and on compatibility issues, and helps developers and software companies to enforce licenses. Till represented the gpl-violations.org project in several lawsuits to enforce the GPL and has published several articles and books related to legal questions of Free and Open Source Software. He was a member of the Committee C in the GPLv3 drafting process.

One thing upfront: I am not a geek. I never have been one, and have no intention of becoming one in the future.

Instead, I am a lawyer. Most people who read this book probably tend to sympathize more with geeks than with lawyers. Nevertheless, I do not want to hide this fact. That the FOSS community is not necessarily fond of lawyers but busy developing software is something I *did* know about FOSS in early 1999 when our ways first crossed. But there were also quite a few things I did not know.

In 1999, while completing my doctoral thesis that focused on a classical copyright topic, I was assessing the scope of moral rights. In this context I spent a while pondering about the question of how moral rights of programmers are safeguarded by the GPL, which allows others to modify their programs. This is how I first got in contact with FOSS. At the time, "free" and "open" certainly had different meanings, but the difference was not worth arguing about in the world I was living in. However, since I was free to do what I was interested in and open to investigate new copyright questions, I soon found out that the two words *do* have something in common, that they are *different* and yet they are best used together...

There are three things I wish I had known back then:

First, my technical knowledge, particularly in the field of software, was insufficient. Second, I did not really know the community and what mattered to the people who were part of it. Last but not least, I did not know much about foreign jurisdictions back then. It would have been useful to know all that from the beginning.

Since that time, I have learned a fair bit, and just as the community is happy to share its achievements I am happy to share my lessons[1]:

Technical knowledge How is software architecture shaped? What is the technical structure of software like? Which licenses are compatible with each other and which are not, and how and why? How is the Linux kernel structured?

To name one example, the important question of what constitutes a "derivative work" according to the GPL determines how the software may be licensed. Everything that counts as derived from GPL-licensed software must be distributed under the GPL. To assess whether a certain software is a "derivative work" or not requires profound technical understanding. The interaction of program modules, linking, IPC, plugins, framework technology, header files and so on determines, among other criteria, whether a program is formally inseparable, which helps to determined whether it is derived from another program or not.

[1] The "Institut für Rechtsfragen der Freien und Open Source Software" (Institute for Legal Questions on Free and Open Source Software) offers, inter alia, a collection of FOSS related literature and court decisions; see www.ifross.org for details.

Knowledge of the industry and the community Besides these functionality issues I had no profound understanding of the idea behind FOSS and the motivation of the developers and the companies that use FOSS. Neither did I really know about its philosophical background, nor was I familiar with practical issues such as "who is a maintainer?" or "how do version control systems work?" In order to serve your clients best, these matters are no less important than your proficiency in technical aspects. Our clients ask us about legal aspects of forming business models such as dual licensing, "open core", support and services contracts, code development and code contribution agreements. We consult clients concerning what FOSS might have in store for their companies or institutions. We also advise developers on what they can do about infringement of their copyrights, and draft and negotiate contracts for them. In order to serve such clients comprehensively, it is important to be familiar with the different points of view.

Comparative law knowledge The third thing a FOSS lawyer needs is knowledge about foreign jurisdictions, at least a few, and the more the better. In order to construe the different licenses, it is essential to be familiar with the perspective of the people who have drafted it. In most cases the U.S. legal system is of key importance. For example, the GPL was drafted with U.S. legal concepts in mind. In the United States, "distribution" includes online distribution, whereas under the German Copyright system there is a distinction between offline and online distribution. Licenses that have been drafted by lawyers from the United States may thus be construed as including online distribution, which might be relevant and helpful in court proceedings[2].

[2] `http://www.ifross.org/Fremdartikel/LGMuenchenUrteil.pdf`, Cf. Welte v. Skype, 2007

Always Learning

So, all this is useful to know. And as software keeps on being developed and modified to provide solutions for the needs of the day, so my mind will hopefully keep on finding answers to the challenges the vibrant FOSS community poses to a lawyer's mind.

42. Building Bridges

Shane Coughlan

Shane Coughlan is an expert in communication methods and business development. He is best known for building bridges between commercial and non-commercial stakeholders in the technology sector. His professional accomplishments include establishing a legal department for the FSFE, the main NGO promoting Free Software in Europe, building a professional network of over 270 legal and technical experts across 27 countries, co-founding a binary code compliance tool project and aligning corporate and community interests to launch the first law review dedicated to Free/Open Source Software. Shane has extensive knowledge of Internet technologies, management best practice, community building and Free/Open Source Software.

When I started to work in Free Software I was struck by the perceived difference between the "community" and the "business" stakeholders in this field. The informal assertion often aired at the time essentially proposed that there were developers interested in hacking and there were commercial parties who would use their output in objectionable ways if not closely monitored. It was a generally baseless assumption, and almost entirely limited to parties who identified themselves as the community rather than those more aligned with business interests, but it was prevalent.

Despite being primarily associated with the community side of things, I resisted the concept that there were two inherently hostile parties facing each other down over the future of Free Software. It sounded too simple to frame the dynamics of contribution, use and support as the interplay between noble creators and devious freeloaders. Indeed, it sounded more like a situation where complexity, change and uncertainty had lead to the creation of simplistic narratives to provide comfort for parties moving out of their comfort zone. I could feel the tension in the air, I could hear the arguments at booths and in meetings, and I could observe the sharp comments or blowing off of steam at conferences. But what did it all mean?

Whether we were talking about Free Software project contribution, project management or license compliance, the relationships between stakeholders were often accompanied by assumptions, lack of communication and negative emotion. This in turn lead to greater complexity and a corresponding increase in the difficulty of making unified decisions or resolving issues. I was aware that one of the biggest challenges was how to build bridges between individuals, projects and businesses, a necessary step to ensure common understanding and cross-communication of the rules, norms and reasons behind the licenses and other formal measures to govern this field, but that in itself does not translate into knowing how to engage with the issue effectively.

This was at the tipping point when GPLv3 was being drafted, Linux-based technology was beginning to appear in all sorts of consumer electronics, and Free Software was at the brink of becoming mainstream. Change was in the air and business investment around major Free Software projects was spiking. Suddenly there were major corporation employees actually doing a lot of the difficult work, there was significant funding available for events, and a lot of the software stopped being about fun, and started to be about milestones, deliverables, quality assurance and usability.

This was probably a system shock to parties who had been doing Free Software for a long time. For much of its evolution Free Software was not just about technical exploration and perfection, but also social interaction. It provided a way for intelligent though occasionally awkward people to share a common interest, to challenge each other, and to cooperate inside carefully delineated and predictable lines. Like stamp collecting, train spotting or Star Trek, it was a place where detail-orientated people could converge, and it had the additional benefit of providing broader feel-good social benefits as an output. It was not where the original contributors had expected to encounter middle-management and output-orientated development focus. No wonder a few noses were out of joint.

And yet... Everything worked out fine. Free Software is everywhere, and appears to be in an almost unassailable position as a mainstream component of the Information Technology industry. Projects like the Linux kernel or the Apache server have continued to grow, to innovate and to attract new stakeholders, both commercial and non-commercial. The balance of power between individuals, projects and businesses changed, occasionally with conflict and disruption, but never at the cost of long-term cooperation or of undermining the core value of Free Software.

From my perspective in the legal field – which after all is merely a formal language that provides a context for interaction through mutually understood and enforceable rules – the tension in Free Software did not lie in the introduction of increased commercial activity, in the increased participation of company employees in projects, or in change itself. The real problem lay in the gap between a displaced previous elite and their newer, occasionally very different, fellow stakeholders.

The challenge was to create a level playing field where the different interests could co-exist with mutual respect. Free Software needed to become a place where information like the proper remit and obligations of a license or requirements for code submissions to a project could be obtained by any party at any time. Subjectivity and vagueness needed to take a backseat to allow the formation of more formalized transactions, which in turn act as an essential precursor for any large economic activity, especially in the context of an international or global community.

What had worked in the early days – be it the trust of a few parties or the common understanding reached by a similar group with similar interests – could no longer act as social or economic drivers for the future of the field. At times this seemed like an insurmountable barrier and that the tensions between the previous contributors to Free Software and new stakeholders must lead to a collapse of cooperation and perhaps of the progress made. But such a grim outcome would presuppose conditions that simply did not exist.

Free Software provided a lot of value to different people and organizations based on some very simple concepts like the freedom to use, modify, improve and share technology. These concepts allowed a great deal of flexibility, and as long as people recognized their value and continued to respect them, challenges over secondary items like project governance or license gray areas were – in the long run – pretty much irrelevant. The rest was mainly noise, the normal communication spike with all its trappings of drama that inevitably occurs when one social group is joined by another. The same applies whether we are talking about a fishing spot, a country welcoming immigrants (or not), or two businesses merging.

The changes in Free Software all looked a little confusing at the time, but essentially break down into three useful lessons that will be familiar to students of history or political science. Firstly, whenever there is an elite, it will seek to preserve its status and it will communicate the perceived challenge as a negative development in an attempt to undermine it. Secondly, despite the inherent tendency of any power base to be conservative, static engagement with a changing field will only result in moving the opportunity for improvement from existing parties to third parties. Finally, if something has value, then challenges in governance are unlikely to undermine that value, but instead will provide a method of refining both the governance mechanisms and the people in a position to apply them.

The development of Free Software as a mainstream technology saw increased professionalization in both the approach of developers and in the management of projects. It also saw greater respect for licenses on the part of individuals, projects and companies. This was no bad thing, and despite a few rocky moments along the way – you can take your pick from inter-community fighting, companies disregarding license terms or the upset caused by a move away from beer and t-shirt culture – we are left with a stronger, more coherent and more valuable field.

And Now it is Your Turn!

I hope you enjoyed our little roadtrip through Free Software. Now it is your turn to do two things:

1. Pass this book on. Share it with someone who would benefit from it.

2. If you are not already contributing to a project start now. Today is the right day. OpenHatch[1] is a great place to start.

— Lydia Pintscher

Karlsruhe, Germany; 4. January 2012

[1] http://openhatch.org

www.ingramcontent.com/pod-product-compliance
Lightning Source LLC
Chambersburg PA
CBHW060824170526
45158CB00001B/69

9781105514937